A FIELD GUIDE TO
SHELLS
OF THE TEXAS COAST

You will also enjoy these Texas Monthly Field Guides:

Wildflowers, Trees & Shrubs of Texas
Delena Tull and George Miller

Archaeological Sites of Texas
Parker Nunley

Birds of the Big Bend
Rolan H. Wauer

Fossils of Texas
Charles Finsley

Reptiles and Amphibians of Texas
Judith M. Garrett and David G. Barker

Stone Artifacts of Texas Indians
Ellen Sue Turner and Thomas R. Hester

Texas Snakes
Alan Tennant

Texas Trees
Benny J. Simpson

Wildlife in Texas and the Southwest
George Oxford Miller

Also of interest:

Beachcomber's Guide to Gulf Coast Marine Life
Nick Fotheringham and Susan L. Brunenmeister

TexasMonthly
FIELDGUIDE
SERIES

A FIELD GUIDE TO
SHELLS
OF THE TEXAS COAST

BY JEAN ANDREWS

Gulf Publishing Company
Houston, Texas

10   9   8   7   6   5   4   3   2   1

Gulf Publishing Company
Book Division
P.O. Box 2608 ☐ Houston, Tx 77252-2608

Library of Congress Cataloging-in-Publication Data
Andrews, Jean.
    A field guide to shells of the Texas coast/ Jean
      Andrews.
      p.   cm. — (Texas Monthly field guide series)
    Originally published: Texas shells. Austin: University
of Texas Press, c1981. (The Elma Dill Russell Spencer
Foundation series; no. 11)
    Includes index.
    ISBN 0-87719-211-1. — **ISBN** 0-87719-210-3 (pbk.)
    1. Shells–Texas–Gulf Region–Identification. 2.
Shells–Texas–Gulf Region–Pictorial works. I. Title.
II. Series.
QL415.T4A63 1992
594'.0471'09764–dc20   91-37622
                                         CIP

Photographs by Jean Bowers Gates.

Contents

Introduction

The United States, perhaps the entire Western World, is on a "shell kick." Buyers at the huge markets of the home, gift, and jewelry trades demand and get everything from 18-karat gold snails carrying rock crystal shells or sterling silver nautilus-shaped wine coolers, to paper napkins and bed sheets adorned with a shell motif. Along with these can be seen crates upon crates of the actual shells which have been fashioned into jewelry and home accessories or used as specimens for display. The shell pattern adorning chinaware, glasses, paper goods, calendars, and other products ad infinitum has been designed to suit any taste— good, bad, or indifferent. It has become so commonplace that one might think a manufacturer had been told, "If it doesn't sell, take it back and put a shell on it."

This urge to collect a shell or to employ shell iconography is not a new trend particular to our modern, cosmopolitan society. Archaeologists and anthropologists have made discoveries giving evidence to ancient use of shells not only for utilitarian purposes but also for aesthetic pleasures. There have been periods throughout history when shell collecting has been more "in" than at other times—for example, the century following the end of the Napoleonic Wars (1815–1915)—but it has never been "out." Today, it is IN! Let us hope

that contemporary collectors will be guided by good conservation practices in collecting so that future collectors will be able to satisfy their innate craving for possession of a sea shell.

Shells come in myriad forms and the sea is not their only home. Limitations of space in a pocket guide prevent elaboration on the variety of shells and the reasons for that variety. This has been explained in any number of books that are available to those who would care to go into the subject in greater depth. One of those is the book from which this field guide is derived, *Shells and Shores of Texas*. That book not only provides details about each specimen and the phylum Mollusca as a whole but also relates much information regarding the history and physical makeup of the Texas coast, as well as when, where, and how to get to the "shelling" areas, and even how to prepare and eat the animals found inside the shells. There are many maps and illustrations designed to facilitate collecting, and an extensive bibliography encompasses the literature in the field.

This guide is intended to be carried to the shore. It concerns the collecting of mollusks from the shallow marine waters of the Texas coast. It includes but a few of those from the deeper waters of the Gulf of Mexico and none that are to be found on land or in streams, rivers, or bodies of fresh water. It is arranged to help both the novice collector and the professional malacologist identify their finds. No keys have been included, because the method of using this guide is simple. Compare your shell with the photographs in the book until you think you have determined your shell's identity. An illustration of each species is placed beside the descriptions, which are arranged systematically beginning with the most primitive and progressing to the higher orders. When a figure is found that resembles the shape and sculpture of your shell, look first at the size category. If the sizes are not comparable, move on.

For illustrations and descriptions of those species listed but undescribed, the reader is referred to the indicated page in *Shells and Shores of Texas (SST)*. Those species are either under 3 mm in size or considered rare in occurrence. The purpose of a field guide is to make possible the identification of plants or animals in the "field" without additional references, microscopes, or dissecting equipment. Like most field guides, this one may fall short of these objectives but we have tried. If there are terms that are unexplained by the diagrams accompanying the text, we apologize and refer you to the extensive glossary in the "parent" book.

Even those readers who don't know a clam shell from a mangrove seed (both appear on the beach in a gaping posture, but the hard chalky one is the bivalve, the other a dicotelyden) need not be told where to look. A stroll along the beach will reward the sharp-eyed beginner with specimens tossed up by the tides. The more seasoned collector will want to gather living specimens. Many mollusks live in the bays in a variety of assemblages—the oyster reef, tidal flats, submerged grass, brackish water, or inlet areas—while others inhabit pilings or jetty rocks, the surf zone, or offshore areas. In Texas the bays and inlets are the most rewarding locations, but it will be a fruitless trip unless accompanied by a low tide. Do not attempt it otherwise. Check tide tables and local newspapers; then plan your shelling expedition to coincide with a minus tide, preferably at full moon following a freeze or "norther" (cold front).

The "sea shell" is the exoskeleton of animals that constitute the Mollusca, a phylum of invertebrates in the animal kingdom. The habitat of these soft-bodied animals is not limited to the sea, nor is a shell present in all the families that make up this group. Many of the 50,000, more or less, molluscan species do not have shells in either their juvenile or adult stages of development. The slimy slug that plagues the gardener has fantastic counterparts in the sea, the nudibranchs, that far outnumber their shelled relatives. In fact, the absence of an external shell is one of the characteristics of the more highly developed orders of mollusks.

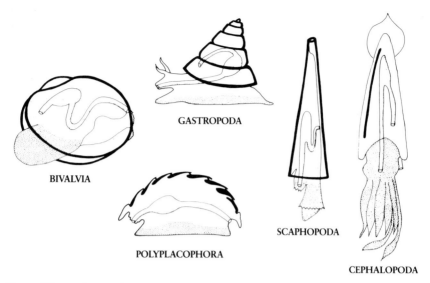

BIVALVIA

GASTROPODA

POLYPLACOPHORA

SCAPHOPODA

CEPHALOPODA

Fig. 1. The molluscan body plan in various classes. The shell is indicated by a heavy line, the digestive tract by small stipples, and the foot by heavier stippling (after R. Buchsbaum, *Animals without Backbones: An Introduction to the Invertebrates* [Chicago: Univ. Chicago Press, 1967]).

It is virtually impossible to generalize the characteristics of recent mollusks because of the enormous diversity of the members of the phylum. The usual concept of a mollusk is that of an animal with a soft, slippery body and a hard shell, but there are many exceptions, for some, such as the octopus and the sea slug, have no adult shell. However, they all have a soft, fleshy body that is referred to in the name Mollusca, "soft bodied."

The various classes of molluscan animals include chitons that cling to rock; clams that burrow, anchor, or skip; snails that float, dig, or climb; the tooth shell that burrows its wide end into the sand; the jet-propelled octopus that slips through the water leaving a smoke screen of ink in its wake; the primitive, wormlike Aplacophora; and the abyssal-dwelling *Neopilina*. They may be found in any habitat—deserts, trees, rivers, lakes, mud, gardens, coral reefs, the depths of the sea, inside or attached to other animals, and buried in the ground. In all of the animal kingdom their variety is rivaled only by the chordates.

The enormous diversity of the Mollusca makes it difficult to formulate a basic pattern that will apply to all members of the group and still be confined to a brief description. They do have certain biological characters that distinguish them from other phyla, but a basic pattern can only be suggested. The unsegmented molluscan body generally contains a variation of three regions: (1) the *head*—sensory-feeding area, (2) the *foot*—locomotor area, and (3) the *visceral hump*—body mass. The tripartite division of the molluscan body is the rule in nearly all mollusks and is not recognizable in any other group of animals. The shell may take many forms or it may be enclosed by the mantle, which is a flap extending from the visceral hump; it may be reduced in size; or it may be completely absent. The shell acts as support or protection for some, but when the shell is nonexistent the animal may develop other means of defense.

Identifying the Shell

One of the most rewarding features of an interest in the field of natural history, whether it be insects, wildflowers, or sea shells, is the pleasure to be had from identifying one's collection. Once collectors are able to name a shell, they can compare their observation of the animal with studies by others. Simply, they can communicate.

Identification of a shell is not always a simple task. A look at illustrations may spot the shell or a near relative so that a reference to the text will point out the real identity. Although the shell of the mollusk may be unsatisfactory as a basis of classification, it is convenient for identification because one seldom has the live animal.

Within a species there might be great variation in color or shape because marine mollusks are extremely responsive to varying environmental conditions. Conversely, some species may be so similar to others that only an anatomical study of the animal will prevent misnomer. Quite often the differences caused by environment are difficult to distinguish from the inherent characteristics of a species.

Standardized names, which can be recognized by students throughout the world, are used to discuss the many kinds of mollusks. Because these names are in international use, Latin or Latinized forms are employed for nomenclature. No one, not even professional malacologists, can remember all of them, but it adds to the pleasure of collecting to be able to recall a few of the more common species.

Like people, a mollusk is given a name of two parts—a binomial. The generic name, always capitalized, is used like the surname, such as Jones or Smith—for example, *Tellina*; the trivial, or specific, name, which is not capitalized and which follows the generic name, corresponds to the first name, such as Jane or George—for example, *texana*. Both of these names are italicized. The name of a person, printed in Roman type, and a date follow the scientific name—for example, *Tellina texana* Dall, 1900—indicating the person who first described the species (the author) and the year in which it was described. If the author's name is in parentheses, it indicates that someone has since studied that particular species and placed it in a different genus from that assigned by the original author. If there is a subgeneric name, it is capitalized and placed in parentheses following the generic name. If there is a subspecific name, it follows the specific name without separation by symbol. Thus, *Genus (Subgenus) species subspecies* Author, date.

Many mollusks have common, or popular, names. These names may vary for the same shell according to region, but in most cases they are names in use by local collectors and fishermen. Many small shells are too little known to have been given a common name.

Until recently much molluscan classification was done on the basis of shell characteristics, but contemporary scientific work emphasizes the study of the organism. The result has been reclassification of many species, and the end is not near. Biologists are becoming aware of unique research potentials and amateurs have an increasing interest in studying the mollusk as a living animal.

Amateurs can make a significant contribution to the science of malacology if they would consider the mollusk as a living animal in a particular environment and record their observations. Record and date your observations, making certain your locality data are accurate by including enough information for a complete stranger to locate the spot on a standard map.

Molluscan Classes

Recent evaluation of the interrelationships of the molluscan classes has caused the introduction of three new subphyla—Aculifera, Placophora, and Conchifera—based on the thesis that all living Mollusca are the offspring of three separate lineages stemming from unrecorded pre-Mollusca. The first subphylum has four known members in the Texas area, the second but two known members; however, the third is represented by five classes encompassing the Texas fauna. The Conchifera is composed of the Monoplacophora (none in Texas) and its four descendant classes—Gastropoda, Bivalvia, Scaphopoda, and Cephalopoda.

CLASS GASTROPODA: SNAILS

The name Gastropoda means "stomach-footed ones." The gastropod shell, which consists of one

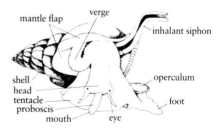

Fig. 2. A coiled gastropod shell with head-foot mass protruded, anterior view (after L. R. Cox, "Gastropoda: General Characteristics of Gastropoda," in *Treatise on Invertebrate Paleontology*, Part I, *Mollusca 1*, ed. R. C. Moore, pp. 184–269 [Boulder, Col.: Geol. Soc. Amer., 1960]; courtesy of the Geological Society of America and the University of Kansas).

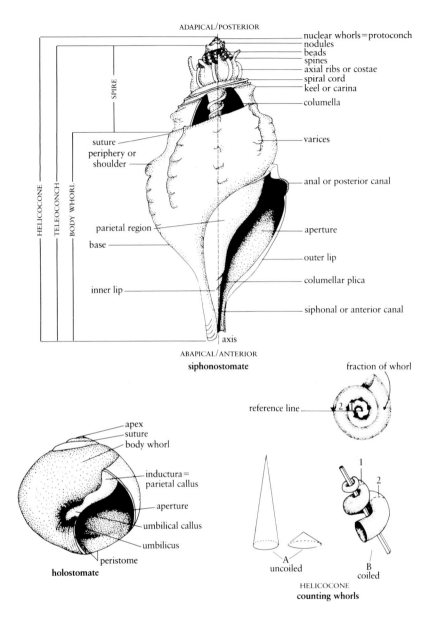

Fig. 3. Parts of the gastropod shell. In this composite shell the columella is seen through a cutaway section. *Counting whorls*: The apical end of the whorl in the diagram is semicircular, with the reference line forming approximate right angles at the sutures. The suture is the line of contact of successive whorls and is perpendicular to the reference line. If there is no coil, there is no whorl, e.g., the limpet. The completion of the first turn is the completion of the first whorl; it does not coincide with the termination of the protoconch. Count counterclockwise from the reference line.

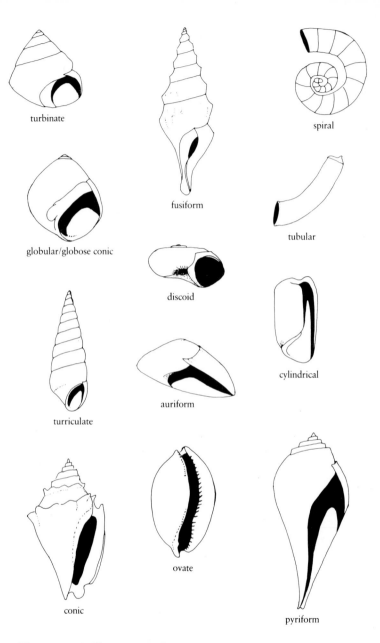

turbinate

spiral

fusiform

tubular

globular/globose conic

discoid

cylindrical

turriculate

auriform

conic

ovate

pyriform

Fig. 4. Diagrammatic illustrations of typical gastropod shell shapes.

unit, is called a univalve. The gastropod is distinct from the other classes of the phylum because of its asymmetrical, spirally coiled, visceral mass and shell. Gastropods are the most diverse group of mollusks. They have adapted for life in both marine and fresh water as well as on land. The primitive forms may browse on algae or minute animals, but others have become scavengers, parasites, and grazers, as well as active carnivorous predators. Adaptations in form probably were based on the requirements of the feeding pattern. Some of the characteristics of the gastropods are illustrated in Figs. 2, 3, and 4.

CLASS BIVALVIA: CLAMS

The Bivalvia (Pelecypoda), or "two-valved ones," contain fewer genera and species than the Gastropods, but in number of individuals they may outweigh all other classes of Mollusca and are the most important economically. All bivalves are aquatic filter feeders on detritus and plankton. Their mode of feeding has limited them to strictly aqueous environments, which can be classified into three habitat categories:
1. *Epifaunal*, normally living exposed above the surface of the substratum
2. *Semi-infaunal*
3. *Infaunal*, normally concealed in the substratum

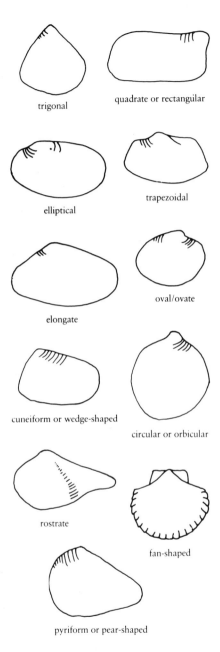

Fig. 5. Diagrammatic illustrations of typical bivalve shell shapes.

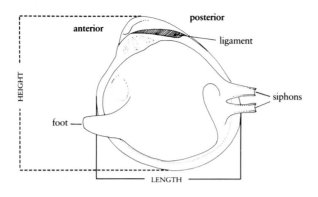

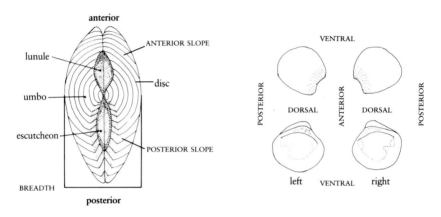

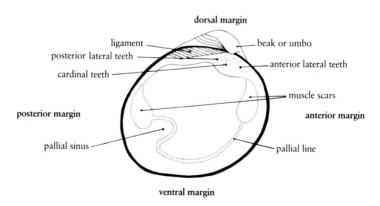

Fig. 6. Parts of the bivalve shell.

The bivalves invariably have two shells, usually external, on either side of the body. Typically, the two valves are of equal convexity (*equivalve*), but in some forms this symmetry has been lost and the valves will differ in size to a varying degree (*inequivalve*). These valves are held together dorsally by a leathery, brown, elastic *ligament*. Some of the characteristics of the bivalves are illustrated in Figs. 5 and 6.

CLASS SCAPHOPODA: TUSKS

The mollusks forming the small class Scaphopoda, "boat footed," burrow with a foot shaped like the prow of a boat. These semi-infaunal marine mollusks feed on detritus and microorganisms with the help of captacula and the foot. The shells are tubular, open at both ends, slightly curved but in one plane, and tapered toward the posterior end. The parts of the scaphopod are shown in Figure 7.

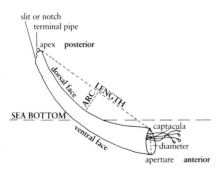

Fig. 7. General features of the Scaphopoda.

CLASS CEPHALOPODA

The Cephalopoda, or "head-footed ones," are the most highly developed of the phylum Mollusca. These strictly marine animals are found in all the oceans of the world. The Octopoda, octopus, and the Decapoda, squid, are the best known members of this class in Texas waters. Both are carnivores that catch their prey with their numerous arms.

CLASS MONOPLACOPHORA

The Monoplacophora are limpet-shaped mollusks long considered extinct. They are not presently known to occur in the Gulf of Mexico.

SUBPHYLUM ACULIFERA

The Aculifera, vermiform, are marine-dwelling mollusks. These deep-water dwellers have only recently been discovered in the Gulf of Mexico. They are shell-less and very small.

SUBPHYLUM PLACOPHORA

The Polyplacophora, or chitons, were formerly grouped with the Monoplacophora in the class Amphineura. The shell has many plates, similar in appearance to that of the garden pill bug. The chiton lives on solid substrata, where it feeds on algae and minute animals. The parts are illustrated in Figure 8.

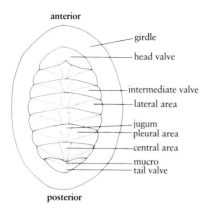

anterior

girdle
head valve
intermediate valve
lateral area
jugum
pleural area
central area
mucro
tail valve

posterior

Fig. 8. General features of the Polyplacophora.

Data Used in the Descriptions

The basis for the present book is knowledge of Texas molluscan life derived from a long period of field work and continued study of the accumulated information available. Collecting over a period of ten years (1960–1970) was confined to the shallow-water, or littoral, fauna and included beach specimens and drift material. Smaller species were obtained by picking through algae and sorting drift material with the aid of a stereomicroscope. No dredging was undertaken. A number of small species and euthyneuras have been omitted from the list due to lack of data, identification, or a suitable specimen to photograph—their omission will not keep the casual collector from being able to identify the shells one is most likely to gather on a Texas beach. Although

nearly 350 species were determined, this in no way implies a complete survey. If the species was collected living, the habitat, together with additional remarks of interest, is given. Many species were not found alive and are indicated as "in beach drift" or "beach shell."

The classification of mollusks is still a matter of debate, and several systems are currently in use. The order used here is basically that of J. Thiele, a standard in the field. The classification of the gastropods is based on a revision in progress by D. W. Taylor and the Siphostomatan [Neogastropod] families of W. F. Ponder. The outline of classification of the bivalves is that of L. McCormick and R. C. Moore. The cephalopods are arranged according to a revision by G. L. Voss.

Some of the abbreviations used in the text are cf. (*confer*), compare; ex gr. (*ex grupo*), of the group of; s.s. (*sensu stricto*), in the strict sense; sp., species; syn. (synonym), other scientific names that have been applied or may apply; and in litt. (*in litteris*), personal communication. A single capital letter in the generic position of a name represents the genus under discussion.

Listing of synonyms has been avoided unless it was felt there was a need for a reference in order to prevent confusion when making comparisons with other popular shell books or recent changes in taxonomy. If a species was first described in a different generic

	Metric		U.S.	
Millimeter (mm)	0.001	m	0.03937	in.
Centimeter (cm)	0.01	m	0.3937	in.
Decimeter (dm)	0.1	m	3.937	in.
Meter (m)	1.0	m	39.37	in.
Kilometer (km)	1,000.0	m	0.6213	mi.
Fathom (fm)	1.829 m		6.0	ft.

combination, the author's name and date of publication appear in parentheses, for example (Say, 1922). In some cases, for the sake of clarity, some former combinations are given in brackets, for example [Cyphoma intermedium].

The size given is the length of an average specimen. Dimensions are given in the metric scale (1 inch = 25.4 mm; 1 foot = 304.8 mm; see table). The general geographic ranges outside Texas are a compilation from published literature. The range in Texas is from both published and unpublished records of collectors known to me, the northernmost listed first, the southernmost last.

Relative abundance, or occurrence, is given according to the occurrence on the beach and does not reflect the quantity to be found where the mollusks live. *Rare, uncommon, fairly common,* and *common* are the categories used. These are subjective estimates, for there are wide variations, and the use of these categories will serve only as a general guide.

Locality is usually designated as east, central, south, or entire. *East* refers to that section of the coast from the Sabine to the Colorado River, where humid and subhumid climates prevail. *Central* is from the Colorado to Padre Island and represents the subhumid river-bay complexes. Padre Island and the Laguna Madre comprise the semiarid *south* region. Some localities overlap more than one region and are therefore described more explicitly; for example, *southern half of coast* indicates from Port O'Connor south. After noting the habitat of the species, the collector will learn that estuarine, or river-influenced, fauna does not occur in the southern range, because no rivers empty into this area; that shelf marine species will not occur naturally in the enclosed bays; and so on. Continued study of the coast is broadening these ranges. With few exceptions, the mollusks described inhabit depths of less than thirty meters. A shell from a location other than Texas was photographed only as a last resort when a good specimen collected in Texas was not available, even though it is well represented in the local fauna. There are less than two dozen examples of this and those were included with regret but with the idea that such a photograph was better than no illustration. All photographed specimens are at the Corpus Christi Museum.

Equipment

Special permits and elaborate equipment are not necessary for collecting in Texas. The seasoned collector usually has favorite essentials, but the beginner will find the following to be handy:

Canvas shoes: broken shell, bottles, and cans buried in the sand can be a hazard to bare feet.

Long-sleeved shirt and pants: even if a tan is desired, the skin can stand only so much.

Mask, snorkle, and diving gear: to look along the jetties.

Notebook and pencil: to record data.

Pill bottles, vials, small cotton bags: for small and special specimens.

Plastic bags: for collecting drift or wrapping messy material.

Plastic bucket: a light-weight carryall.

Pockets: either built-in or added apron fashion.

Small strainer or wire-bottomed boxes: for sifting shells from sand and mud.

Sun glasses: the glare on the white sand and the water is blinding.

Sun hat: the Texas sun can produce painful burns even on a cloudy day.

Thread or string: to tie valves together.

Trowel: for digging in the sand and mud or lifting the layer of drift from the sand.

Tweezer or toothpicks: to pick up minute shells (wet the end of the toothpick).

Waders, rubber boots, and thermal underwear: since winter brings the best collecting, these items will make the northers bearable.

Cleaning

Cleaning your shell is of great importance, since a beautiful specimen, improperly preserved, can quickly become an unlovely thing. First, consider the mollusk that is taken alive.

Many types of mollusks may be cleaned by simply boiling them and then removing the soft parts. Start them in cold water with a folded piece of cloth on the bottom of the pan to reduce breakage. Boil slowly until the flesh is firm or the clam has opened. Cool to lukewarm before washing. Boil only a few shells at a time and remove the bodies immediately when cool enough to handle because cooling causes the body to contract and shrink up into the shell. A corkscrew motion will usually get all the soft parts from the winding snail shell. If the visceral portion of the body breaks off, a few drops of 5 percent formalin (formaldehyde gas dissolved in water) placed in the shell will eliminate bad odors. The formalin should then be removed; no shell should be stored in a solution of formaldehyde, because of the destructive action it has on the shell itself. Dental tools, nut picks, and wires are handy for the body-removing operation.

Some highly polished shells like *Strombus*, *Oliva*, or *Cypraea* will craze if boiled. The animals in porcelaneous shells can be killed by placing them in fresh water. Most can then be picked clean, but some are stubborn. These may be dehydrated in the refrigerator. Wrap each shell in a paper towel with extra thickness next to the aperture and place with the aperture down in the refrigerator for a week. At this time the animal should come out easily. If it does not, do not soak it in anything, for this type of shell waterspots easily. Dry it carefully and allow it to sit with the aperture up until the remaining animal has dried up and can be shaken out.

The true collector wants to preserve the operculum or "trap door" of the operculate shell. Not all snails have an operculum, but they are an interesting feature of many. Mark them in some way so that you keep the correct operculum with its own shell. When these have been dried, they may be glued in their natural position after the thoroughly clean shell has been stuffed with cotton.

Tiny snails are best preserved by allowing them to remain out of water until they die (fresh water will cause them to withdraw far into the shell) and then placing them in a solution of 70 percent ethyl, or grain, alcohol or 50 percent methyl or isopropyl alcohol. If they are placed directly in the alcohol, the animal will contract and draw the operculum into a position where it will not be visible. After several days in the solution the small snail shells may be drained and spread to dry before storing.

The bivalves or clams are cleaned in the same way, taking care not to break the ligament that holds the two sections together. Many collectors prefer that the shell be dried closed in its natural position. After the soft parts are removed, cotton string is wrapped around the closed valves until the ligament dries. Rubber bands, adhesive tape, and other tapes may prove disastrous. Heat causes the rubber to melt and the adhesive coating on the tape comes off, leaving a hard-to-remove residue on the once-beautiful shell. Other collectors prefer that the bivalve be dried in a butterfly position so that the interior is visible. If one is fortunate enough to have several specimens, it is desirable to dry the clam in both positions. William J. Clench, an editor of *Johnsonia*, recommended preserving bivalves in a solution of four parts alcohol and one part glycerine to keep the periostracum and ligament soft and pliable. An occasional dab of glycerine on the ligament will prevent it from becoming brittle.

The fastidious collector may want to clean off all the foreign matter that is attached to the outside of the shell. This again is a matter of taste, as many desire their shells in the natural state with the exterior uncleaned. It is a good idea to have an example of a cleaned and an uncleaned shell in your collection because cleaning often reveals hidden beauty.

A stiff brush is usually enough to do the job of cleaning. Growth that cannot be removed with the brush can often be removed with a sharp pointed instrument, such as an awl, a knife, or a dental tool. The limey deposits can prove quite stubborn and often one must resort to muriatic acid. Experience has proved that this job must be done with running water at hand. The shell is held with forceps and *quickly* dipped into full-strength acid, then immediately held under running water. Extreme caution must be used with this method. The acid is a poison and can burn your skin. Use it only as a last resort. Apertures and delicate parts of the shell can be coated with melted paraffin to protect them from the acid. Shells overcleaned with acid take on an unnatural sheen and can be spotted a yard away in a shell shop. The composition of shells varies; some will withstand the acid and others, like the lion's paw, will dissolve immediately when put in contact with the powerful caustic.

The exterior may also be cleaned with ethyl acetate, a chemical which will not attack the calcium carbonate. It is purchased by the gallon from chemical companies.

Often the shell is covered with vegetation and sponge that can be removed by the use of household chlorine compounds. The chlorine will not dissolve the calcium of the shell as do muriatic acid and formalin, but it does have a tendency to bleach the shell if contact is maintained over too long a period. (A note from experience: extended use of chlorine will dissolve your fingernails.)

The following method is not recommended as an enjoyable pastime, but in some cases it may prove necessary. Delicate shells like the purple sea snail may be cleaned by "watering." Place them overnight in fresh water and then rinse away the fleshy parts. This procedure may need to be repeated several times. A word of warning— change the water daily or more often. The decomposition of the animal's body forms corrosives that dull the surface of the shell if it is allowed to remain in the same water for too long a period.

After the shell is cleaned, its natural luster may be restored by rubbing a thin coating of some type of greasy substance on it. Vegetable fats become sticky with age; it is best to use mineral oil, baby oil, or vaseline. Store oiled shells in closed cabinets to avoid the accumulation of dust on the coated surfaces.

Most collectors shudder at the thought of a shell that has been coated with varnish or shellac or overcleaned with acids. Don't kill the shell with kindness. A shell carefully cleaned to preserve its natural beauty can be a joy forever.

A word on traveling with a collection of live caught specimens; you may develop your own method but until you do let me recommend a method learned the hard way. Leave the animal in the shell and wrap the individual shell with newspaper, protecting the lip with extra thickness and stuffing the aperture firmly. If paper towels or tissue are available, they work well for the stuffing. Place the wrapped shell in a plastic bag and tie tightly. Plastic garbage-can liners are good for putting several wrapped specimens together and are stronger than smaller bags. Small specimens may be packed in plastic jars in a 30 percent alcohol solution. Carry the whole mess in a garbage can with a tightly fitting lid and cover the top lightly with plastic before putting the lid on. Plan to bring the materials you will use with you from home. Not every place has newspaper. Decomposition of sea life, especially in the Texas climate, is rapid and odorous. In other words, it will stink quickly.

One trip without proper preparation will be enough. A return trip from the west coast of Mexico was ghastly; even the customs agents passed our car without coming near to examine it, waving us on as quickly as possible.

Preserving

In some instances it may be desirable to relax the animal so that its soft parts are preserved in a lifelike manner without excessive contraction or distortion. Magnesium chloride is the anesthetic most highly recommended for marine animals. Try 75 grams of $MgCl_2$ in a liter of fresh water mixed with an equal volume of sea water. If the animal has not been in the solution for more than twelve hours, it may be revived in normal sea water. However, the most readily available material for relaxing is menthol crystals. A few crystals of menthol are added to the water covering the mollusks in a small bottle. Two or three drops of a saturated solution of menthol in 95 percent alcohol may be used. The specimens should be kept cool and undisturbed while being narcotized. After several hours (6 to 48, depending on the number and size of the animals and the volume of water used), to be sure the specimens are insensitive to strong stimuli, such as probing, one or two should be carefully tested in the killing fluid before the entire lot is transferred. It is well to leave them in the menthol for an hour after they become insensitive to the stimuli. If they are left too long, however, the tissue will deteriorate, making the specimens useless for micromorphological studies. When the snails are fully relaxed, the water should be replaced with 5 percent formalin.

After a day or so, they can be transferred to 70 percent alcohol. To preserve color in nudibranchs and other opisthobranchs, use an anti-oxidant (Ionol C.P.-40) 0.3 percent by volume in a solution of 5 percent formalin in sea water. A data label must accompany each lot of cleaned specimens.

Storing

The storing of a sea shell collection presents special problems. Although properly cleaned sea shells do not deteriorate, they do tend to fade in direct sunlight and extreme heat. This feature, combined with their variety of size and shape, makes the shell collection hard to store.

There are several types of collections—the whatnot shelf, the display cabinet, the study collection, the aquarium, and the photograph collection. The first is usually the outcome of a summer's beachcombing by the beginner or it may be an auxiliary to the study collection. The second is generally found in museums, clubs, libraries, and even homes. It is planned for visual appeal, is not overcrowded, is well labeled, has good lighting, and contains choice specimens. The study collection is housed more compactly, with the catalog number, scientific name, date found, and location recorded for each specimen.

In a study collection it is essential to record carefully the depth of water, special conditions, occurrence, substratum, and date when the specimen was secured. A shell that cannot be given a definite locality adds no value to a collection. (Not just "Texas" but "beach drift, near jetties, Port Aransas, Nueces Co., Texas.")

The importance of locality data cannot be overemphasized. Much of the potentially valuable material I collected as a novice was unwittingly lost to science because of improper or careless locality information. Do not trust your memory—jot it down. Distribution maps of the area in which you are collecting can be made by placing dots on standard maps. Without maps, the locality should be accurate to within a quarter of a mile. An example of the importance of this information—in order to avoid frustrating and time-consuming search—is a paper which cited *Busycon perversum* as being from "Obregón, Mexico." The *International Atlas* showed the only two Obregón's to be inland towns. It was not until much valuable time had elapsed that it was determined that the location cited was intended to refer to the fishing port near the Yucatán Peninsula—Puerto Alvaro Obregón, Tabasco, Mexico.

Small plastic pill bottles and gelatin capsules are handy for storing the smaller specimens and may be obtained in a variety of sizes from your pharmacist. Labels made on biological paper withstand time as well as liquid preservatives.

Corrugated paper linings in the storage drawers will prevent small bottles and vials from rolling about. Modular plastic boxes with a plastic container to hold a group of them can be ordered from Althor Products, American Hinge Corp., 946 Danbury Rd., Wilton, CT 06897. This company's catalog illustrates a great many types of plastic containers. The tiny shells are best housed in slides. I prefer the micropaleontological slides with glass covers and metal slide holders that can be ordered from Curtin Matheson Scientific Inc., Labcraft, 9999 Veteran's Memorial Dr., Houston, TX 77038.

Larger specimens can be stored in drawers with small boxes for dividers. Avoid the use of cotton because it clings to rough surfaces and is difficult to remove. A little more trouble but worthwhile is lining the drawers with a thick (dependent on drawer depth and shell thickness) layer of foam rubber or styrofoam. Using an X-acto knife or razor blade, cut a berth to house each individual shell. The drawer is beautiful to look at and chipping is kept to a minimum because the shells never touch each other or jiggle around.

A catalog list in a notebook or a card file is a necessity to prevent the loss of the valuable locality data. You will want to record the precise location, the date, and many other data. The method of collection is important, too. Not all this information can be attached to each shell, hence a numbering system must be used for ease in locating the recorded data. Whatever system is used, you will assign to each shell a specific number. This number can be written in an inconspicuous place on the larger shells with india ink and a fine pen. The Rapidograph pen is excellent for this job and for recording in your catalog or notebook. Water will not smear dry india ink. A shell too small to write on can have its number affixed to the slide or container.

I prefer the double-entry type of catalog, but it is only one of many systems. With it, acquisitions are first entered as received, the number is placed on the shell or its container. Separate localities may be indicated by letters that are added to the numbers. The second entry is in an alphabetical listing of the genera. Care must be taken to allow space between the names for future additions. The numbers are entered opposite the individual species but are not consecutive. Use a loose leaf notebook for this catalog.

Shell Condition

Shell collectors who exchange shells or purchase shells like to know what they are getting. A set of international shell-grading standards has been agreed upon to guide such exchanges.

GEM   A perfect specimen of an adult shell. Gastropods have their correct operculum and periostracum. Bivalves have both valves.

FINE   Only minor flaws on an adult shell. Clean, no repairs.

GOOD   May be sub-adult with few flaws, and exhibit the characteristic of the species. Clean.

POOR   A beach specimen. Faded or worn, with some damage.

JUVENILE   Immature.

W/O   With original operculum in gem quality shell. For other categories, an operculum of the same species.

FULL DATA   Detailed information concerning habitat, date of collection, location, collector.

BASIC DATA   Place collected, collector/dealer, year collected.

Texas Shells
A Field Guide

Phylum MOLLUSCA Cuvier, 1795

Subphylum ACULIFERA Hatscheck, 1891

Class APLACOPHORA Von Ihering, 1876

The members of the class Aplacophora are minute, deep-water organisms without shells that the average collector cannot expect to find, but their recent collection and identification by Granville Treece is such a significant addition to the molluscan fauna of the Gulf of Mexico that they are listed. They will not be found in *Shells and Shores of Texas* because they have been discovered since its publication.

Order CHAETODERMATIDA
  Simroth, 1893
Family RIMIFOSSORIDAE
  Salvini-Plawen, 1968

Genus *Scutopus* Salvini-Plawen, 1968

Scutopus ventrolineatus
  Salvini-Plawen, 1968

Family CHAETODERMATIDAE
  Von Ihering, 1876

Genus *Falcidens* Salvini-Plawen, 1968

Falcidens sp.

Family PROCHAETODERMATIDAE
  Salvini-Plawen, 1968

Genus *Prochaetoderma* Thiele, 1902

Prochaetoderma sp.

Class SOLENGASTRES Gegenbaur, 1878

Family PARARRHOPALIDAE
  Salvini-Plawen, 1882

Genus *Pruvotina* Cockerell, 1903

Pruvotina impexa (Pruvot, 1890)

Subphylum PLACOPHORA Von Ihering, 1876

Class POLYPLACOPHORA Blainville, 1816 = [AMPHINEURA Von Ihering, 1876, in part]

Order NEOLORICATA
  Bergenhayn, 1955
Suborder ISCHNOCHITONINA
  Bergenhayn, 1930
Family ISCHNOCHITONIDAE
  Dall, 1889

Genus *Ischnochiton* Gray, 1847

Mesh-Pitted Chiton
Ischnochiton papillosus
  (C. B. Adams, 1845)

Size: 8–12 mm.
Color: Whitish, mottled with olive green.
Shape: Oval.
Ornament or sculpture: Girdle narrow, alternately white and olive; upper surfaces of valves sculptured with microscopic pittings; end valves with concentric rows of fine, low beads; lateral areas with fine, sinuous, longitudinal lines; posterior valve concave with 9 slits.
Habitat: High-salinity lagoons on shell and reefs; offshore.
Localities: Entire.
Occurrence: Fairly common.
Range: Tampa to lower Keys; Texas; West Indies.
Remarks: Under old shell in bays.

Subfamily CHAETOPLEURINAE
  Plate, 1899

Genus *Chaetopleura*
  Shuttleworth, 1853

Chaetopleura apiculata (Say, 1839)

Size: 7–20 mm.
Color: Variable from ashy gray or brown to buff; interior white or grayish.
Shape: Oval.
Ornament or sculpture: Dorsum carinate; intermediate valves with well-marked oblique lines separating central area from lateral area which bear numerous rounded beads; girdle narrow, mottled, with scattered transparent hairs.
Habitat: High-salinity lagoons on jetty and reef.
Localities: Entire.
Occurrence: Uncommon.
Range: Cape Cod; both sides of Florida; Texas.
Remarks: More common offshore. Fifth valve broken in figured specimen.

Subphylum CONCHIFERA Gegenbaur, 1878

Class MONOPLACOPHORA Wenz, 1940

To date no member of this class has been found living in the Gulf of Mexico.

Class GASTROPODA Cuvier, 1797

Subclass PROSOBRANCHIA
Milne Edwards, 1848 = [STREPTO-
NEURA Spengel, 1881]
Infraclass DIOTOCARDIA Mörch,
1865 = [ARCHAEOGASTROPODA
Thiele, 1925]
Order RHIPIDOGLOSSA Mörch, 1865
Suborder ZEUGOBRANCHIA
Von Ihering, 1876
Superfamily FISSURELLACEA
Fleming, 1822
Family FISSURELLIDAE Fleming, 1822
Subfamily DIODORINAE
Odhner, 1932

Genus *Diodora* Gray, 1821

Keyhole Limpet
Diodora cayenensis (Lamarck, 1822)

Size: 25–51 mm.
Color: Varies from pinkish, whitish, to dark gray; interior white or blue gray, polished.
Shape: Conic, oblong oval; rather thick shell; like coolie hat.
Ornament or sculpture: Orifice keyhole-shaped, just in front of and slightly lower than apex; every fourth rib noticeably larger; ribs crossed by concentric, lamellar ridges.
Aperture: Oval with heavy callus; margins irregularly and finely crenulated; interior smooth.
Habitat: Intertidal to moderately deep water; mainly on underside of rocks, jetties; attached epifaunal.
Localities: Entire.

Occurrence: Uncommon in east, becoming common south to Mexico.
Range: Bermuda; Maryland to southern half of Florida; Texas; Gulf of Mexico to Quintana Roo; Surinam; Brazil.
Remarks: Algal covering on live specimens makes finding difficult.

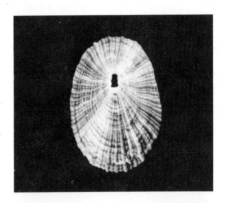

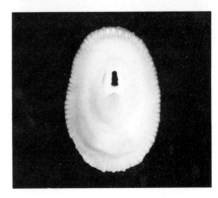

5

Genus *Lucapinella* Pilsbry, 1890

File Fleshy Limpet
Lucapinella limatula (Reeve, 1850)

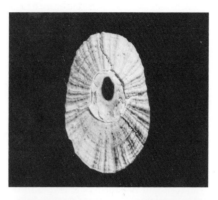

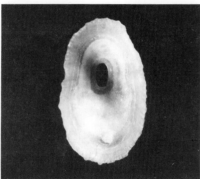

Suborder AZYGOBRANCHIA
  Spengel, 1881
Superfamily TROCHACEA Rafinesque,
  1815
Family TROCHIDAE Rafinesque, 1815
Subfamily CALLIOSTOMATINAE
  Thiele, 1921

Genus *Calliostoma* Swainson, 1840
Subgenus *Kombologion* Clench &
  Turner, 1960

Sculptured Top-Shell
Calliostoma (Kombologion) euglyptum
  (A. Adams, 1854) [See *SST*, p. 73]

Subfamily MONODONTINAE
  Cossmann, 1916

Genus *Tegula* Lesson, 1835

Smooth Atlantic Tegula
Tegula fasciata (Born, 1778)

Size: 15 mm.
Color: Dull white with brownish
mottlings.
Shape: Oblong conic; almost central
apical hole.
Ornament or sculpture: Radial ribs
alternately large and small; growth
lines form concentric lamellations, or
scales, as they cross ribs.
Aperture: Large; interior smooth,
white, porcelaneous; callus rounded,
smooth, with crenulate margins.
Habitat: On rocks, jetties, oyster reefs;
attached epifaunal.
Localities: Port Aransas, south.
Occurrence: Uncommon.
Range: North Carolina to southern half
of Florida; Texas; Yucatán; West
Indies; Brazil.
Remarks: Lives entirely underwater.

Size: Width 12–18 mm.
Color: Background light or reddish
brown; mottled with reds, browns,
blacks, white; callus and umbilicus
white.
Shape: Turbinate.
Ornament or sculpture: 12 postnuclear
whorls sculptured with 3 or more fine
spiral threads; umbilicus deep, round,
smooth.

Aperture: Rounded with 2 teeth at base of columella.
Habitat: On *Thalassia* grass and algae in shallow water; epifaunal.
Localities: Entire, more to south.
Occurrence: Common in beach drift.
Range: Southeastern Florida; Texas; Gulf of Mexico to Quintana Roo; Costa Rica; West Indies to Brazil.
Remarks: To date, not reported alive on Texas coast, although old shells abundant in bay drift around Port Isabel and Port Aransas; worn specimen typical.

Family PHASIANELLIDAE Swainson, 1840

Genus *Tricolia* Risso, 1826

Checkered Pheasant
Tricolia affinis cruenta Robertson, 1958

Size: 6.2 mm.
Color: Background white or pale orange patterned with spiral rows of squarish, dark red spots.
Shape: Inflated, conic.
Ornament or sculpture: 4½ smooth, rounded whorls; apex rounded; suture impressed; umbilicus only a chink.
Aperture: Elongate ovate; columella with thick, white callus; outer lip smooth.

Habitat: Shallow bays on algae; epifaunal.
Localities: San José Island, south.
Occurrence: Fairly common.
Range: Texas; Yucatán; Quintana Roo; Caribbean coast of Central America; northern South America; Brazil; sporadic along western Gulf of Mexico.
Remarks: This herbivore may be plant specific.

Suborder PLANILABIATA Stoliczka, 1868
Superfamily NERITACEA Rafinesque, 1815
Family NERITIDAE Rafinesque, 1815

Genus *Nerita* Linné, 1758

Antillean Nerite
Nerita fulgurans Gmelin, 1791

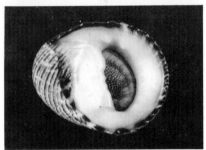

Size: 18–25 mm.
Color: Dark gray to black with occasional blurred markings.
Shape: Globose conic; body whorl expanded, spire low.
Ornament or sculpture: Strong spiral cords; heavy shell.

Aperture: Large, rounded with 2 prominent teeth on inside of outer lip; inner lip yellowish white, toothed, with decklike, porcelaneous callus.
Habitat: Marine; jetties and pilings near high-tide mark; epifaunal.
Localities: Port Aransas, south.
Occurrence: Uncommon.
Range: Southeastern Florida; Texas; Yucatán; Costa Rica; West Indies; northeastern Brazil.
Remarks: Newcomer to Texas with jetties; can live around 75 days out of water. Places eggs on own shell or those of other mollusks; also look for *N. tessellata* Gmelin, 1791, recently collected alive on Brazos de Santiago jetties (it is mottled).

Genus *Neritina* Lamarck, 1816
Subgenus *Vitta* Mörch, 1852

Olive Nerite
Neritina (Vitta) reclivata (Say, 1822)
[See *SST*, p. 75]

Virgin Nerite
Neritina (Vitta) virginea (Linné, 1758)

Size: 4–12 mm.
Color: Color and pattern variable: background olive, white, gray, red, yellow, purple, or black with black and/or white waves, stripes, dots, lines, or mottlings.

Shape: Globular with expanded body whorl.
Ornament or sculpture: Smooth, polished.
Aperture: Semilunar; parietal area smooth, convex, white to yellow, with variable number of small, irregular teeth.
Habitat: Bay margins and grass flats; epifaunal.
Localities: Entire.
Occurrence: Common, more to south.
Range: Bermuda; Florida to Texas; Gulf of Mexico to Quintana Roo; Costa Rica; West Indies; Surinam; almost all of Brazilian coast.
Remarks: Lays eggs in winter on own shell or that of other mollusks; eggs are in clustered, yellowish, gelatinous capsules; patterns so varied one might think each a different species; more colorful in brackish water than in more saline water; photosensitive.

Genus *Smaragdia* (Maury, 1917)

Emerald Nerite
Smaragdia viridis viridemaris (Maury, 1917)

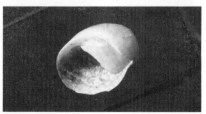

Size: 6–16 mm.
Color: Bright pea green with few fine, broken white lines near apex; these

outlined in maroon color in some specimens.

Shape: Obliquely oval, subglobular, low spire.

Ornament or sculpture: Glossy, smooth.

Aperture: Simple, semilunar; outer lip thin, sharp; parietal area green with 7 to 9 minute teeth.

Habitat: Grass flats in shallow bays; epifaunal.

Localities: Port Aransas, south.

Occurrence: Uncommon.

Range: Bermuda; southeastern Florida; Texas; Gulf of Mexico to Quintana Roo; Costa Rica; West Indies.

Remarks: Animal green; first reported living in Texas by me; photosensitive.

Infraclass MONOTOCARDIA Mörch, 1865 = [CAENOGASTROPODA Cox, 1959]
Order CTENOBRANCHIA Schweigger, 1820 = [PECTINIBRANCHIA Blainville, 1814]
Suborder HOLOSTOMATA Fleming, 1828
Superfamily LITTORINACEA Gray, 1840
Family LITTORINIDAE Gray, 1840
Subfamily LITTORININAE Gray, 1840

Genus *Littorina* Férussac, 1821
Subgenus *Littorinopsis* Mörch, 1876

Angulate Periwinkle
Littorina (Littorinopsis) angulifera (Lamarck, 1822)

Size: 25–30 mm.

Color: Background varies: bluish white, orange yellow, dull yellow, reddish brown, or grayish brown.

Shape: Conic with elongate spire; higher than wide.

Ornament or sculpture: Darker elongated spots on ribs, often fused to form oblique stripes on body whorl;

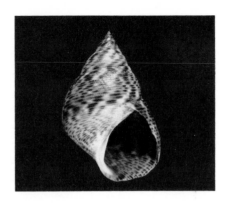

early whorls have regularly spaced, vertical white spots below suture; about 6 convex whorls, body whorl about one-half of height; slightly channeled sutures; spiral sculpture of irregular, inequidistant incised lines; anomphalous.

Aperture: Rounded oval; outer lip smooth, does not flare, sharp and nearly horizontal at body whorl; inner lip with thin deposit over body whorl; columellar area smooth, moderately wide, with central groove in lower portion.

Habitat: Brackish water; mangrove thickets, on black mangrove, *Avicennia nitida* (subject to freeze in this area); climbs high into tree and can spend much time out of water; at times on pilings and rocks; epifaunal.

Localities: On rocks at Corpus Christi Naval Air Station and Port Isabel area.

Occurrence: Uncommon.

Range: Bermuda; southern half of Florida; Texas; West Indies; Brazil; Pacific Panama; central west Africa.

Remarks: After hard freezes this species disappears.

Marsh Periwinkle
Littorina (Littorinopsis) irrorata (Say, 1822)

Subgenus *Austrolittorina* Rosewater, 1970

Zebra Periwinkle
Littorina (Austrolittorina) lineolata Orbigny, 1840

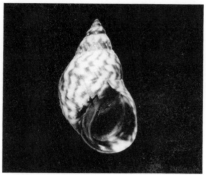

Size: 25 mm.
Color: Grayish white with tiny, short streaks of reddish brown on spiral ridges; opaque, dull.
Shape: Elongate conic; longer than wide.
Ornament or sculpture: 8 to 10 gradually increasing, flat whorls; suture weak; body whorl about one-half of total height; numerous, regularly shaped spiral grooves; shell thick.
Aperture: Oval; columella and callus usually pale reddish brown; outer lip stout, sharp, with tiny, regular grooves on inside edge.
Habitat: On marsh grass in low-salinity bays; epifaunal.
Localities: East, central.
Occurrence: Common.
Range: New Jersey to central Florida to Texas.
Remarks: Herbivorous on algae; when tide out, animal withdraws into shell, which may remain dry and exposed to sun for many hours; often completely out of water on stems of marsh grass where it leaves a mucus trail.

Size: 12–25 mm.
Color: Background gray with oblique zigzag lines of dark brown; apex reddish brown.
Shape: Elongate conic.
Ornament or sculpture: 6 to 8 gradually increasing convex whorls; body whorl more than one-half of total height, more convex than other whorls; suture well marked; male smaller and more strongly sculptured with spiral grooves than female.
Aperture: Pear-shaped; outer lip not flaring, edge sharp and thin; meets body whorl at sharp angle; columellar area long, wide, slanting inward, smooth; anomphalous; purple to mahogany brown.
Habitat: Intertidal on rocks, jetties, pilings; often in large colonies in crevices; epifaunal.
Localities: Entire.
Occurrence: Common.
Range: Bermuda; southern half of Florida to Texas; Costa Rica; Brazil.
Remarks: Has been misidentified as *L. ziczac* (Gmelin, 1790) in Texas. *L. lineolata* darker in color, smaller, and with a wider apical angle.

Subgenus *Littoraria* Gray, 1834

Cloudy Periwinkle
Littorina (Littoraria) nebulosa
(Lamarck, 1822)

Size: 15 mm.
Color: Background bone yellow or white with bluish tinge; early whorls have spotting of white and reddish brown, which stops abruptly on sixth or seventh whorl; variable in juveniles.
Shape: Elongate conic.
Ornament or sculpture: 7 to 9 gradually increasing convex whorls; body whorl about two-thirds of total height; nuclear whorls usually eroded in adults; suture well marked, smooth or slightly crenulate behind outer lip; spiral engraved lines become evident on fourth whorl, becoming numerous and more regularly spaced on body whorl; strong transverse striations cross spiral lines at angles.
Aperture: Subcircular; outer lip not flaring; edge thin, sharp, smooth, meeting body whorl at sharp angle; slight callus over body whorl, columella long, wide, smooth; anomphalous; mouth yellowish brown to pale purplish within; outer lip whitish; columella white.
Habitat: Pilings and jetties in more saline waters; epifaunal.
Localities: Entire.
Occurrence: Fairly common.
Range: Bermuda; Texas; Caribbean coast of Central America; West Indies; northern South America; Pacific Panama.
Remarks: Prefers wooden jetties, wreckage, and logs; avoids rocks exposed to heavy surf; seldom survives Texas winters; numbers greatly reduced since killing freeze of 1962.

Subgenus *Melarhaphe* Menke, 1828

Spotted Periwinkle
Littorina (Melarhaphe) meleagris
(Potiez & Michaud, 1838) [See *SST*, p. 80]

Superfamily RISSOACEA Gray, 1847
Family RISSOIDAE Gray, 1847
Subfamily RISSOINAE Gray, 1847

Genus *Swartziella* Nevil, 1884

Catesby's Risso
Swartziella catesbyana Orbigny, 1842

Size: 3–5 mm.
Color: Shiny white.
Shape: Elongate conic.
Ornament or sculpture: 8 whorls, slightly rounded; suture fairly deep; about 14 strong ribs to each whorl.

Aperture: Oval, slightly oblique; strong tooth on inner side of outer lip.
Habitat: *Thalassia* grass beds in brackish, shallow, inshore waters; epifaunal.
Localities: Entire.
Occurrence: Fairly common in beach drift.
Range: Bermuda; North Carolina; Florida; Texas; Gulf of Campeche; Campeche Bank; Quintana Roo; Costa Rica; West Indies; Brazil.
Remarks: Pronounced "riss-o-ee-na"; *R. chesneli* Michaud, 1830, of authors. [*Rissoina. chesneli* Michaud, 1830, of authors].

Genus *Zebina* H. & A. Adams, 1854

Smooth Risso
Zebina browniana (Orbigny, 1842)

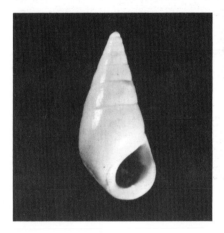

Size: 4 mm.
Color: Shiny white or pale amber.
Shape: Elongate conic.
Ornament or sculpture: 9 to 10 slightly convex whorls, smooth; suture shallow; apex small, prominent.
Aperture: Oval, entire; outer lip thickened.
Habitat: Under shell and debris in grassy bottom beyond littoral zone; epifaunal.
Localities: Entire.
Occurrence: Common in beach drift.
Range: Bermuda; North Carolina to

Gulf of Mexico; Texas to Quintana Roo; Costa Rica; West Indies.
Remarks: Syn. *Rissoina laevigata* (C. B. Adams, 1850); [*R. browniana*].

Family ASSIMINEIDAE H. &. A. Adams, 1856

Genus *Assiminea* Fleming, 1828
Assiminea cf. *A. succinea* Pfeiffer, 1840

Size: 5 mm.
Color: Pale brown, translucent.
Shape: Conic.
Ornament or sculpture: No ornament other than microscopic striae; 5 to 5¾ whorls; regularly rounded, sutures shallow.
Aperture: Pyriform, simple; inductura overlaps preceding whorl; anomphalous.
Habitat: Salt marshes with moisture and protection from sun; lives just out of water; epifaunal.
Localities: Entire.
Occurrence: Common.
Range: Boston to Texas; Quintana Roo; Brazil.
Remarks: Quantities living on flats just north of high bridge at Corpus Christi, Texas, in 1973.

Family LITTORIDINIDAE Thiele, 1929

Genus *Texadina* Abbott & Ladd, 1951

Texadina barretti (Morrison, 1965)
[See *SST*, p. 82]

Texadina sphinctostoma (Abbott &
Ladd, 1951) [See *SST*, p. 83]

Family HYDROBIIDAE Troschel, 1857

Genus *Probythenella* Thiele, 1928

Probythenella louisianae (Morrison,
1965)

Size: 3.3 mm.
Color: Polished, translucent.
Shape: Elongate ovate.
Ornament or sculpture: 4½ slightly
convex whorls, separated by distinct
but very shallow suture, microscopically spirally striate, and with
minute growth lines; spire narrowly
obtuse, first 3 whorls rapidly increasing; last whorl deflected, increasing
rapidly only in height, almost three-
fourths shell height, and abruptly constricted at aperture; entire shell appears
subcylindrical, or pupiform; abrupt
(downward) constriction of last whorl
at aperture causes heavy variciform
thickening of lip to appear to fill
upper angle of whorl, producing almost evenly elliptic peritreme in adults.

Aperture: Entire, slightly oblique;
umbilicus narrow, distinct slit.
Habitat: Brackish water; epifaunal.
Localities: Entire.
Occurrence: Common.
Range: Louisiana; Texas.
Remarks: Syn. *Vioscalba louisianae*;
Probythenella protera Pilsbry, 1953, a
fossil.

Family TRUNCATELLIDAE Gray,
1840
Subfamily TRUNCATELLINAE Gray,
1840

Genus *Truncatella* Risso, 1826

Truncatella caribaeensis Reeve, 1842

Size: 5.5–7.5 mm.
Color: White to pale amber, shiny.
Shape: Elongate conic.
Ornament or sculpture: 4 to 4½
convex whorls; deeply impressed
suture; 17 or more poorly developed
transverse costae, some specimens may
be nearly smooth; costae appear only
on upper part of whorl; mature
specimens appear very different from
young due to loss of early whorls.
Aperture: Ovate, somewhat flaring,
entire; angled above and rounded
below; outer lip simple, thin, thickened
at union with body whorl; columella
not apparent; anomphalous.

Habitat: In bays above high-tide and inlet areas; epifaunal but under wet debris.
Localities: Entire.
Occurrence: Fairly common.
Range: Bermuda; southeastern United States; Texas; Carmen, Campeche, Mexico; Gulf of Campeche; Quintana Roo; West Indies; northeastern Brazil.
Remarks: Formerly misidentified in Texas as *T. pulchella* Pfeiffer, 1839; out of water in damp spots under driftwood along bay margins.

Family VITRINELLIDAE Bush, 1897

Genus *Vitrinella* C. B. Adams, 1850

Vitrinella cf. *floridana* Pilsbry & McGinty, 1946

Size: 1.8 mm.
Color: White.
Shape: Slightly turbinate.
Ornament or sculpture: Umbilicus broadly open; protoconch slightly elevated; 2 postnuclear whorls; prior whorls can be seen; walls convex.
Aperture: Circular, oblique; columella slightly thickened.
Habitat: Inlet-influenced areas and near shore; epifaunal.
Localities: Entire.
Occurrence: Fairly common in beach drift.
Range: Southern Florida and Texas to Campeche Bank; Quintana Roo.
Remarks: Uncarinated umbilicus differentiates this from *V. helicoidea.* [Figures in *SST*, p. 86, are of two different specimens of *V. floridana.*]

Helix Vitrinella
Vitrinella helicoidea C. B. Adams, 1850 [See *SST*, p. 86]

Genus *Cyclostremiscus* Pilsbry & Olsson, 1945
Subgenus *Ponocyclus* Pilsbry, 1953

Jeanne's Vitrinella
Cyclostremiscus (Ponocyclus) jeaneae Pilsbry & McGinty, 1946 [See *SST*, p. 87]

Trilix Vitrinella
Cyclostremiscus (Ponocyclus) pentagonus (Gabb, 1873) [See *SST*, p. 88]

Cyclostremiscus (Ponocyclus) suppressus (Dall, 1889) [See *SST*, p. 88]

Genus *Anticlimax* Pilsbry & McGinty, 1946
Subgenus *Subclimax* Pilsbry & Olsson, 1950

Anticlimax (Subclimax) pilsbryi (McGinty, 1945)

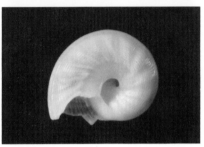

Remarks: Callus-filled umbilicus causes confusion with the *Teinostoma;* look for zigzag grooving.

Genus *Episcynia* Mörch, 1875

Hairy Vitrinella
Episcynia inornata (Orbigny, 1842)

Size: 3.4 mm.
Color: White.
Shape: Discoid, spire slightly dome-shaped.
Ornament or sculpture: 2½ postnuclear whorls sculptured with numerous, fine zigzag spiral grooves; more grooves on dorsal side than on base; periphery just above base marked with strong keel; umbilicus partly filled with heavy callus, may be entirely filled.
Aperture: Oblique; lip slightly thickened in adults; parietal callus thick, on preceding whorl.
Habitat: On muddy bottom in shallow water; shore; epifaunal.
Localities: Entire.
Occurrence: Fairly common in beach drift.
Range: Southern Florida; Texas; Quintana Roo.

Size: 3.4 mm.
Color: White, glassy.
Shape: Trochiform.
Ornament or sculpture: 4½ postnuclear whorls sculptured with narrow peripheral keel fringed with minute projecting teeth; umbilicus narrow, flat-sided, deep with stepped appearance.
Aperture: Flattened oval; lip incomplete.
Habitat: Offshore and along shore; epifaunal.
Localities: Port Aransas, south.
Occurrence: Uncommon in beach drift.
Range: Texas; Campeche Bank; Greater Antilles.
Remarks: Peripheral sculpture jewellike.

Genus *Parviturboides* Pilsbry & McGinty, 1950

?Parviturboides interruptus (C. B. Adams, 1850) [See *SST*, p. 90]

Genus *Solariorbis* Conrad, 1865
Subgenus *Solariorbis* s.s.

Solariorbis (Solariorbis) blakei Rehder, 1944

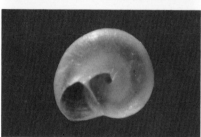

Size: 1.45 mm.
Color: White.
Shape: Discoid.
Ornament or sculpture: 1½ postnuclear whorls sculptured with microscopic spiral grooves and brief transverse wrinkles fanning from suture; suture only slightly impressed; nuclear whorls project slightly; base broad, smooth, evenly rounded; umbilicus may be nearly or entirely closed but always a narrow chink and never looks like *Teinostoma*.
Aperture: Oblique, rounded; parietal callus extends beyond aperture.
Habitat: Inlets and bays; epifaunal.
Localities: Entire.
Occurrence: Fairly common in beach drift.

Range: Eastern coast of United States; Florida; Gulf states; Mexico.
Remarks: Thickening around umbilicus most distinctive characteristic of genus. [Specimens figured in *SST*, p. 90, are *Vitrinella floridana* Pilsbry & McGinty, 1946.]

Solariorbis (Solariorbis) infracarinata Gabb, 1881 [See *SST*, p. 91]

Solariorbis (Solariorbis) mooreana Vanatta, 1903 [See *SST*, p. 91]

Genus *Pleuromalaxis* Pilsbry & McGinty, 1945

Bales' False Dial
Pleuromalaxis balesi Pilsbry & McGinty, 1945 [See *SST*, p. 93]

Subfamily TEINOSTOMATINAE Cossmann, 1917

Genus *Pseudorotella* Fischer, 1987

Tiny-Calloused Teinostoma
Pseudorotella parvicallum Pilsbry & McGinty, 1945 [See SST, p. 94]

Genus *Teinostoma* H. & A. Adams, 1854

Teinostoma cf. *bicaynesne* Pilsbry & McGinty, 1945 [See *SST*, p. 93]

Family CAECIDAE Gray, 1850

Genus *Caecum* Fleming, 1813
Subgenus *Micranellum* Bartsch, 1920
Beautiful Little Caecum
Caecum (Micranellum) pulchellum (Stimpson, 1851) [See *SST*, p. 95]

Subgenus *Elephantulum* Carpenter,
 1857

Cooper's Caecum
Caecum (Elephantulum) imbricatum
 Carpenter, 1858

Size: 4–5 mm.
Color: Glossy, opaque, white.
Shape: Curved, tubular.
Ornament or sculpture: Longitudinal
sculpture of about 24 rounded ribs
crossed by numerous rings; more
prominent near aperture, giving
cancellate appearance; apical plug has
prong to one side; fairly heavy shell.
Aperture: Round.
Habitat: Offshore on sand and shell
banks.
Localities: Port Aransas, south.
Occurrence: Uncommon in beach drift.

Range: South of Cape Cod to northern
Florida and Texas; Campeche Bank;
Quintana Roo; Bahamas; West Indies.
Remarks: Syn. *C. cooperi* (S. Smith,
1870); most caecums feed on diatoms
and detrital particles in algal thickets in
well-lighted zone on rocks, gravel,
sand, and mud.

Subgenus *Brochina* Gray, 1857

Johnson's Caecum
Caecum (Brochina) johnsoni Winkley,
 1908

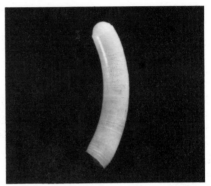

Size: 4.5 mm.
Color: White.
Shape: Curved, tubular.
Ornament or sculpture: Shell narrow,
thin, smooth, subdiaphanous; aperture
not contracted or tumid, white; septum
without appendage.
Aperture: Circular, not constricted.
Habitat: Bays and oyster reefs;
epifaunal.
Localities: Entire.
Occurrence: Common in beach drift.
Range: Europe; North Carolina to
Florida; Texas.
Remarks: First reported for Texas by
Hulings (1955); lays eggs in capsules
attached to bottom; often confused
with *C. glabrum* Montagu, 1803, a
European species.

17

Subgenus *Meioceras* Carpenter, 1858

Little Horn Caecum
Caecum (Meioceras) nitidum Stimpson,
1851

(protoconch, first stage)

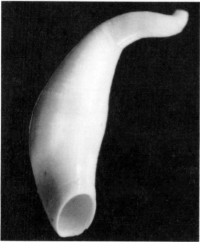

(second and third stages still joined)

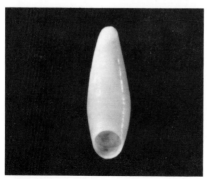

(adult, third stage)

Size: 2.5 mm.
Color: Shiny white or brownish with irregular mottlings of opaque white.
Shape: Tubular with swollen center.
Ornament or sculpture: Smooth, polished; apical plug convexly rounded with tiny projection to one side.
Aperture: Round, oblique, sharp edged; larger than apical end.
Habitat: Intertidal; epifaunal.
Localities: South.
Occurrence: Fairly common in beach drift.
Range: Southern half of Florida; Texas; Quintana Roo; West Indies; northeastern Brazil.
Remarks: According to D. R. Moore (in litt.), the center figure shows the second and third stages of growth after the protoconch drops off: "The second stage usually drops off when the third stage is about half grown. However, in some areas, especially Aransas Bay, the second stage is retained with all three stages. The septum that seals the posterior end of the shell forms before drop-off. After the septum is formed, the poorly calcified line that marks the separation point is no longer in contact with living tissue. This area then begins to deteriorate and allows separation of the two stages."

Superfamily TORNACEA Kuroda,
   Habe, & Oyama, 1971
Family TORNIDAE Sacco, 1896

Genus *Macromphalina* Cossmann,
   1888

Macromphalina palmalitoris Pilsbry &
   McGinty, 1950 [See *SST*, p. 97]

Genus *Cochliolepis* Stimpson, 1858

Cochliolepis parasitica Stimpson, 1858

Cochliolepis striata Dall, 1889

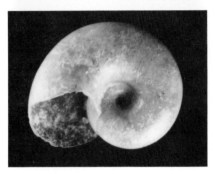

Size: 3.55 mm.
Color: White, glassy.
Shape: Discoid.
Ornament or sculpture: 2 postnuclear whorls smooth except for occasional growth line; spire flat and partially covered with thin callus of shell from each successive whorl; umbilicus shallow, broadly open.
Aperture: Oblique; lip incomplete; parietal callus thin.
Habitat: Shallow coastal bay; commensal with worm; epifaunal.
Localities: Entire, more to south.
Occurrence: Uncommon in beach drift.
Range: Beaufort, North Carolina; Charleston, South Carolina; western coast of Florida; Texas.
Remarks: Heavy growth lines give nautiloid appearance; animal red; syn. *C. nautiliformis* (Holmes, 1860); herbivore, or detritus feeder, which lives commensally with tube worm *Polydontes lupina.*

Size: 6.5 mm.
Color: White.
Shape: Discoid.
Ornament or sculpture: Thin shell has 4 whorls sculptured with numerous spiral striations; base smooth, but umbilicus striated; first nuclear whorl slightly projecting, while remainder covered by thin callus from succeeding whorls; umbilicus slightly constricted.
Aperture: Oblique; lip thin, incomplete; no parietal callus.
Habitat: Shallow coastal bays; probably commensal with a worm; epifaunal.
Localities: Entire.
Occurrence: Uncommon in beach drift.
Range: North Carolina to Caribbean; western coast of Florida; Texas.
Remarks: Will probably be reclassified into another family and genus.

Superfamily ARCHITECTONICACEA
Gray, 1850
Family ARCHITECTONICIDAE Gray,
1850

Genus *Heliacus* Orbigny, 1842

Orbigny's Sundial
Heliacus bisulcata (Orbigny, 1842)
[See *STT*, p. 99]

Genus *Architectonica* Röding, 1798

Common Sundial
Architectonica nobilis (Röding, 1798)

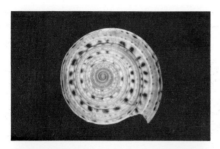

Aperture: Subquadrate; lip thin,
irregularly crenulated; interior white.
Habitat: Along shore with sea pansies;
epifaunal.
Localities: Entire.
Occurrence: Common.
Range: Southeastern United States to
West Indies; Texas; Campeche Bank;
Surinam; all of Brazilian coast; western
Mexico to Peru; eastern Pacific.
Remarks: Miocene species that survives
on both sides of Panama; syn. *A. granulata* (Lamarck, 1816); usually buried
shallowly in sand with adapical part
pointing into sand, opposite to most
prosobranchs; nocturnal, feeding on
soft-bodied actinian-type coelenterates.

Superfamily TURRITELLACEA
Woodward, 1851
Family VERMETIDAE Rafinesque,
1815
Subfamily VERMICULARIINAE
Kimoshita, 1932

Genus *Vermicularia* Lamarck, 1799

West Indian Worm Shell
Vermicularia cf. *V. spirata* Philippi,
1836

Size: 25–51 mm.
Color: Background cream with orange
brown spots spirally arranged, more
prominent next to suture;
porcelaneous.
Shape: Broadly conic; spire low.
Ornament or sculpture: Early whorls
marked with spiral cords that appear
beaded due to growth lines of spire; 4
or 5 prominent sulcations and traces of
others on remaining whorls; base flat,
more strongly sculptured than topside;
umbilicus deep, wide, surrounded with
strongly crenulated spiral cord.

Size: 18–25 mm.
Color: Light brown, paler toward
aperture.
Shape: Very elongate conic or
turriculate.

Ornament or sculpture: About 6 regular whorls closely coiled; later whorls detached, giving a wormlike appearance; about 3 spiral cords form keels at sutures of later whorls; weak, irregular transverse growth lines; fine spiral threads between major cords.
Aperture: Round, thin lipped.
Habitat: Intertidal, attached to rocks, in mud, in bays; attached epifaunal.
Localities: Entire, more to south.
Occurrence: Common in beach drift.
Range: Southeastern Florida; Texas; Carmen, Campeche, Mexico; Yucatán; Quintana Roo; Caribbean.
Remarks: No live specimens reported in recent years, but vast quantities of shells occur along bay shores of southern half; syn. *V. fargoi* Olsson, 1951.

Superfamily CERITHIACEA Fleming, 1822
Family MODULIDAE Fischer, 1884

Genus *Modulus* Gray, 1842

Atlantic Modulus
Modulus modulus (Linné, 1758)

Size: Height 12 mm.
Color: Grayish white spotted with brown.
Shape: Turbinate.
Ornament or sculpture: About 3 small whorls in spire; body whorl large with sloping shoulders and keeled base;

upper portion of shell marked with low spiral ridges and oblique, transverse growth lines; five strong cords on base; umbilicus deep, small.
Aperture: Round with thin, slightly crenulated outer lip that is thickened and marked with low ridges within; white, porcelaneous; columella short with distinctive single tooth near base.
Habitat: On *Thalassia* grass; intertidal; epifaunal.
Localities: Entire, more to south.
Occurrence: Common in beach drift.
Range: Bermuda; Florida Keys to West Indies; Texas; Gulf of Mexico to Quintana Roo; Costa Rica; almost all of Brazilian coast.
Remarks: No live specimens reported in recent years; abundant shells along Aransas ship channel all badly worn as is figured specimen.

Family POTAMIDIDAE
  H. & A. Adams, 1854
Subfamily POTAMIDINAE
  H. & A. Adams, 1854

Genus *Cerithidea* Swainson, 1840
Subgenus *Cerithideopsis* Thiele, 1929

Plicate Horn Shell
Cerithidea (Cerithideopsis) pliculosa (Menke, 1829)

Size: 25.6 mm.
Color: Dark brown or brownish black with bone yellow varices; sometimes grayish yellow spiral band through middle of whorls.
Shape: High conic or turriculate with siphonal notch.
Ornament or sculpture: 11 to 13 slightly convex whorls; unevenly spaced transverse ribs, 18 to 25 per whorl; many fine, uneven spiral striations; on body whorl ribs stop below periphery at strong cord; 6 to 9 spiral cords continue over base; 5 to 8 prominent varices characteristic feature of adult, usually beginning with sixth whorl.
Aperture: Subcircular; outer margin convex, columellar margin concave; shallow indentation at base near columella for siphon; outer lip greatly thickened, forming raised, rounded varix.
Habitat: Mud flats in bays; semi-epifaunal.
Localities: Entire.
Occurrence: Common.
Range: Louisiana; Texas; Yucatán; West Indies.
Remarks: Juvenile specimens without strongly developed varices easily confused with other ceriths; before Hurricane Beulah in 1967, could be seen crawling on mud flats of Aransas Bay at low tide, but huge influx of fresh water resulting from storm decimated population; returning in Portland area; a favorite food of water birds.

Family CERITHIIDAE Fleming, 1822
Subfamily CERITHIINAE Fleming, 1822

Genus *Cerithium* Bruguière, 1789
Subgenus *Thericium* ('Rochebrune') Monterosato, 1890

Florida Cerith
Cerithium (Thericium) atratum (Born, 1778)

Size: 37 mm.
Color: White with narrow, spiral brown bands.
Shape: Elongate conic or turriculate with siphonal canal.
Ornament or sculpture: 11 to 13 slightly convex whorls; 2 to 3 white former varices on each whorl; several rows of beaded spiral cords on each whorl with finer granulated cords separating them; beads fairly regular, giving neat appearance.
Aperture: Oval, oblique; outer lip thickened into crenulated varix; parietal area glossy white; anterior siphonal canal short and upturned; posterior canal simple fold where lip joins body whorl.
Habitat: Littoral, on sea grasses; epifaunal.
Localities: Entire.
Occurrence: Uncommon beach shell.
Range: North Carolina to southern half

of Florida; Texas; Yucatán; northeastern and eastern Brazil.
Remarks: To date, none reported living in Texas; probably fossil; syn. *C. floridanum* Mörch, 1876.

Muddy Cerith
Cerithium (Thericium) lutosum
  (Menke, 1828)

Size: 6–12 mm.
Color: Brown black or grayish white with mottlings of reddish brown; nuclear whorls whitish.
Shape: Elongate conic, turriculate.
Ornament or sculpture: 8 slightly convex whorls; sutures distinct; 7 to 8 beaded, spiral cords on body whorl interspaced with fine striations; repeated but fewer in number on remaining whorls; 1 to 2 former varices on each whorl.
Aperture: Oval; outer lip thin on edge with thickened varix behind edge; parietal area white and glossy but thin; columella short, edged in white with brief upturned siphonal canal; only slight posterior canal.
Habitat: Littoral, on algae and marine grass; in shallow bays; semi-epifaunal.
Localities: Central, south.
Occurrence: Common.

Range: Bermuda; southern Florida; Texas; Gulf of Mexico to Quintana Roo; Costa Rica; West Indies.
Remarks: Syn. *C. variabile* (C. B. Adams, 1845); found on *Thalassia* grass and crawling along mud flats of Aransas Pass area; more abundant in summer; animal black with white mottlings; eyes behind base of tentacles; secretes mucus thread to suspend itself; lays eggs in gelatinous strings.

Subfamily DIASTOMATINAE
  Cossmann, 1895

Genus *Diastoma* DeShayes, 1850

Variable Bittium
Diastoma varium (Pfeiffer, 1840)

Size: 5–6 mm.
Color: Grayish brown.
Shape: Elongate conic, turriculate.
Ornament or sculpture: 7 to 8 slightly convex whorls, sutures definite; numerous rounded, curved transverse ribs crossed by spiral grooves that give nodulose appearance to sculpture; base has spiral grooves but no ribs.
Aperture: Oval, thin with varix adjacent; anterior siphonal canal poorly developed.
Habitat: On marine grass; in bays; epifaunal.

Localities: Entire.
Occurrence: Common.
Range: Maryland to Florida; Texas to Gulf of Campeche; Yucatán; Quintana Roo; Costa Rica; West Indies; Brazil.
Remarks: During warm months collected in vast numbers from blades of marine grass in Aransas Bay; eggs tiny, deposited in gelatinous string coiled into counterclockwise spiral; larvae planktrophic; food for drum; [*Bittium varium* Pfeiffer, 1840].

Genus *Alabina* Dall, 1902

Miniature Horn Shell
Alabina cerithidioides (Dall, 1889)

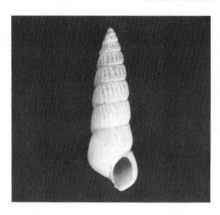

Size: 2–4 mm.
Color: Cream to light brown.
Shape: Elongate conic.
Ornament or sculpture: 8 to 10 whorls, first 3 smooth; remaining whorls with narrow, curved axial ribs and faint revolving threads.
Aperture: Somewhat rounded, outer lip thin; columella weakly curved and ending in slight lip below, behind which is small narrow umbilicus.
Habitat: Inlet areas; epifaunal.
Localities: Entire, more to south.
Occurrence: Common in beach drift.
Range: Florida; Texas; Campeche Bank; Quintana Roo; West Indies.

Remarks: Difficult to separate from *Diastoma varium* and juvenile *Cerithium lutosum;* [*Finella cerithidioides*]; *Finella dubia* (Orbigny, 1842) may be syn.

Superfamily CERITHIOPSIODEA
Family CERITHIOPSIDAE H. & A. Adams, 1854

Genus *Cerithiopsis* Forbes & Hanley, 1849

Green's Miniature Cerith
Cerithiopsis greeni (C. B. Adams, 1839)

Size: 3 mm.
Color: Glossy brown.
Shape: Elongate conic, turriculate.
Ornament or sculpture: 9 to 12 convex whorls; nuclear whorls smooth; remaining whorls with 3 rows of glassy beads joined by spiral and transverse threads.
Aperture: Oval, lip thin; columella arched in juveniles but straight with slight, flaring anterior notch in adults.
Habitat: Bays, inlets, shelly sand; epifaunal.
Localities: Entire.
Occurrence: Fairly common in beach drift.
Range: Bermuda; Cape Cod to both sides of Florida and Texas; Gulf of Mexico to Quintana Roo; Costa Rica.
Remarks: Lives on marine plants; confused with *Diastoma* but whorls are more convex and siphonal canal better developed.

Genus *Eumetula* Thiele, 1912

Awl Miniature Cerith
Eumetula emersoni (C.B. Adams, 1838)

Genus *Seila* A. Adams, 1861

Adams' Miniature Cerith
Seila adamsi (H. C. Lea, 1845)

Size: 12–18 mm.
Color: Light brown with suture sometimes darker.
Shape: Slender, elongate conic, awl-shaped.
Ornament or sculpture: 10 to 14 flat-sided whorls, sutures distinct; 3 strong spiral rows of raised, roundish beads, revolving thread between beaded rows; faint axial ribs may connect beads; middle row of beads less prominent than others; base concave with cordlike spiral ridges and fine transverse growth lines.
Aperture: Oval; lip thin; short, slightly flared anterior siphonal canal.
Habitat: Inlet, shelly sand along shore; epifaunal.
Localities: Central, south.
Occurrence: Uncommon in beach drift.
Range: Massachusetts to West Indies; Texas; Costa Rica.
Remarks: [*Cerithiopsis emersonii*]. Syn. *C. subulata* (Montagu, 1808). Looks like elongated *C. greeni* at first glance. Offshore.

Size: 10 mm.
Color: Brown.
Shape: Elongate conic, nearly cylindrical.
Ornament or sculpture: About 12 flat-sided whorls, regularly increasing in size; 3 strong, flattened spiral ridges on each whorl; concave spaces between them marked with fine spiral striations and delicate transverse lines that do not cross ridges; base of shell concave.
Aperture: Oval; outer lip crenulated to correspond with external sculpture; columella short, ending in centrally located siphonal canal, slightly recurved.
Habitat: Under old shell in hypersaline bays and inlets; epifaunal.
Localities: Entire.
Occurrence: Fairly common.
Range: Bermuda; Massachusetts to Florida; Texas; Carmen, Campeche, Mexico; Gulf of Campeche; Campeche Bank; Yucatán; Costa Rica; West Indies; Brazil.
Remarks: Found in Aransas Bay by turning broken shell and examining attached algae; chalky and bleached when dead.

Genus *Epitonium* Röding, 1798
Subgenus *Epitonium* s.s.

White Wentletrap
Epitonium (Epitonium) albidum
  (Orbigny, 1842)

Size: 20 mm.
Color: Shiny white.
Shape: Elongate conic, turriculate.
Ornament or sculpture: 9 to 11
gradually increasing, moderately
convex whorls, attached by costae only;
bladelike transverse costae rather low
and generally fused with costae on
previous whorl; body whorl contains
12 to 14 unangled costae; may have
microscopic spiral threads but not
strong enough to be grouped with
those considered to have spiral
striations; anomphalous.
Aperture: Subcircular; outer lip
expanded, reflected; parietal area
narrow, slightly thickened, held away
from body whorl by costae; nearly
holostomatous.
Habitat: Intertidal to 360 meters (200
fathoms); epifaunal.
Localities: Entire.
Occurrence: Fairly common in beach
drift.
Range: Bermuda; southern Florida;
Texas; Costa Rica; West Indies;
Surinam; south to northern Argentina;
west Africa.

Remarks: Low ribs appear to form
continuous oblique lines bottom to top.

Angulate Wentletrap
Epitonium (Epitonium) angulatum
  (Say, 1831)

Size: 19–25 mm.
Color: Glossy white.
Shape: Elongate conic, turriculate.
Ornament or sculpture: 8 moderately
convex whorls gradually increasing in
size from apex; sculpture on whorls of
numerous reflected, bladelike costae;
costae form angles on shoulder of each
whorl, stronger on early whorls, a little
less to almost absent on later whorls;
costae in line with those on whorl
above and fused where they meet;
anomphalous.
Aperture: Subcircular; outer lip
thickened, held away from body whorls
by costae; columella not defined.
Habitat: Intertidal to moderate depths
with sea anemones; epifaunal.
Localities: Entire.
Occurrence: Common in beach drift.
Range: Bermuda; eastern end of Long
Island to Florida (excluding lower
Keys); Texas; Brazil.
Remarks: Some specimens more slender
than typical form and can be confused
with *E. humphreysi* (Kiener); juvenile

shell more strongly angulated than adult; as shell reaches maturity, costae become more thickened and rounded.

Humphrey's Wentletrap
Epitonium (Epitonium) cf.
   E. humphreysi (Kiener, 1838)

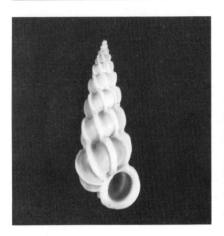

Size: 12–20 mm.
Color: Flat white.
Shape: Elongate conic, turriculate.
Ornament or sculpture: 9 to 10 strongly convex whorls; numerous bladelike to rounded costae on whorls, also serve to connect whorls; suture deep; costae more bladelike on early whorls, becoming thickened and rounded with maturity; may be reflected and angled at whorl shoulder, especially on early whorls; body whorl has 8 to 9 costae; anomphalous.
Aperture: Subcircular; outer lip expanded; usually thickened; parietal lip thin, tightly pressed to body whorl; columella short, arched.
Habitat: Inlet areas and along shore on sandy bottoms; epifaunal.
Localities: Entire.
Occurrence: Fairly common in beach drift.
Range: Cape Cod south to Florida (not lower Keys) and west to Texas; Carmen, Campeche, Mexico.

Remarks: Difficult to distinguish from *E. angulatum* (Say); if typical, more narrow, costae more rounded, less developed shoulder angle but very variable.

Tollin's Wentletrap
Epitonium (Epitonium) cf. *E. tollini*
   Bartsch, 1938

Size: 14 mm.
Color: White.
Shape: Elongate conic, turriculate.
Ornament or sculpture: 9 to 10 convex whorls that can be adpressed or separated and attached by costae only; numerous bladelike costae, 11 to 16 on body whorl; costae spaced irregularly, not always lined up with those on whorl above; even in height throughout with occasional thick one, especially on body whorl; not angled at shoulder, and no spiral sculpture; suture deep; anomphalous.
Aperture: Subcircular; outer lip thickened, reflected; parietal area thin, pressed closely to body wall; columella short, arched.
Habitat: Probably intertidal; epifaunal.
Localities: Entire.
Occurrence: Common in beach drift.
Range: Western Florida from Marco Island north to Gasparilla Island; Texas.

Remarks: Look for mismatched costae and occasional large one; most common *Epitonium* in northern part of range, less so to south.

Subgenus *Gyroscala* Boury, 1887

Brown-Banded Wentletrap
Epitonium (Gyroscala) rupicola (Kurtz, 1860)

Size: 12–20 mm.
Color: White to cream with 2 brownish, spiral bands at suture; costae white.
Shape: Elongate conic, turriculate.
Ornament or sculpture: 11 globose whorls attached at sutures; suture deep; transverse sculpture consists of numerous low, bladelike costae, interspersed with rounded varices; height and number of costae variable, not lined up with costae on adjoining whorl; basal ridge well defined with thin, threadlike line.
Aperture: Subcircular; lip slightly thickened, reflected; nearly entire.
Habitat: Below low water to 36 meters (20 fathoms); epifaunal.
Localities: Entire.
Occurrence: Fairly common in beach drift.
Range: Massachusetts south to Florida and west to Texas; Surinam.
Remarks: Look for brown bands.

Subgenus *Asperiscala* Boury, 1909

Dall's Wentletrap
Epitonium (Asperiscala) cf.
  E. apiculatum (Dall, 1889)

Size: 4.5 mm.
Color: White.
Shape: Elongate conic, turriculate.
Ornament or sculpture: 9 convex whorls attached by costae only; axial sculpture consists of numerous bladelike costae; 11 costae on body whorl; nuclear whorls smooth; first 3 postnuclear whorls possess costae which are low, cordlike, and far more numerous than those on remaining whorls; spiral, threadlike cord only on first 3 postnuclear whorls; later whorls have strong bladelike costae.
Aperture: Circular with thickened, expanded lip; umbilical area partially closed by parietal thickening; columella short, arched.
Habitat: Probably along shore; epifaunal.
Localities: Entire.
Occurrence: Uncommon in beach drift.
Range: South Carolina; Texas; Puerto Rico.
Remarks: Could be aberrant form of some other species, which may explain limited distribution.

Multiribbed Wentletrap
Epitonium (Asperiscala) multistriatum
(Say, 1826)

New England Wentletrap
Epitonium (Asperiscala) novangliae
(Couthouy, 1838)

Size: 15 mm.
Color: White.
Shape: Elongate conic, turriculate.
Ornament or sculpture: 8 to 10 strongly convex whorls, later ones unattached; suture deep; transverse sculpture consists of very numerous cordlike to low bladelike costae not angled at shoulder; many finely incised lines between these that do not cross ribs; apical whorls much smaller in proportion to later ones and have more ribs; anomphalous.
Aperture: More oval than round with very narrowly expanded lip; columella not defined; parietal lip tightly pressed to parietal area.
Habitat: Offshore; epifaunal.
Localities: Entire.
Occurrence: Common in beach drift.
Range: Bermuda; Massachusetts south to Cape Canaveral and west to Texas; Brazil.
Remarks: Many ribs and more delicate appearance than other *Epitonium* make identification easy.

Size: 14 mm.
Color: White, banded with light brown above and below periphery of whorl; often light brown throughout.
Shape: Elongate conic, turriculate.
Ornament or sculpture: 8 to 10 strongly convex whorls gradually increasing in size from apex, later whorls attached by costae only; numerous bladelike to cordlike costae, latter as a result of costae being reflected back and down; body whorl has 9 to 16 costae angled or hooked at shoulder; spiral sculpture reticulated pattern formed by numerous spiral threads crossed by finer transverse lines; no basal ridge.
Aperture: Subcircular with narrow expanded lip; parietal lip only moderately thickened, pressed to body whorl above umbilicus.
Habitat: Offshore; epifaunal.
Localities: Entire.
Occurrence: Common in beach drift.
Range: Bermuda; Massachusetts; Virginia south to Campeche Bank; Brazil.
Remarks: Most common *Epitonium* on southern Padre Island.

Epitonium (Aperiscala) sericifilum
 (Dall, 1889)

Genus *Depressiscala* Boury, 1909

Depressiscala nautlae (Mörch, 1874)
 [See *SST*, p. 113]

Family JANTHINIDAE Leach, 1823

Genus *Janthina* Röding, 1798
Subgenus *Jodina* Mörch, 1860

Dwarf Purple Sea Snail
Janthina (Jodina) globosa Blainville,
 1822

Size: 5.1–10 mm.
Color: Mat white.
Shape: Slender, elongate conic,
turriculate.
Ornament or sculpture: 10 convex
whorls, gradually increasing from apex;
suture moderately defined; transverse
costae numerous, oblique, low; spiral
threads numerous but do not cross
costae; no basal ridge; anomphalous.
Aperture: Subcircular; outer lip slightly
thickened; no parietal shield.
Habitat: Inlet areas; epifaunal.
Localities: Entire.
Occurrence: Uncommon in beach drift.
Range: Texas; Honduras.
Remarks: Easily recognized by close,
oblique ribs and angled periphery of
whorls; lip of figured specimen broken.

Size: 6–19 mm.
Color: Deep violet.
Shape: Globose ovate.
Ornament or sculpture: Thin shell
faintly striated, with striae following
edge of aperture; at indentation of
latter they curve, forming distinct keel
on last whorl.
Aperture: Outer lip deeply indented at
mid-whorl point.
Habitat: Pelagic.
Localities: Entire.
Occurrence: Uncommon.
Range: Worldwide.
Remarks: Float comparatively small;
egg cases of this hermaphrodite pear-
shaped and contain about 75 eggs; syn.
J. umblicata Orbigny, 1940; "*J. exigua
Lamarck*" of authors, not Lamarck,
1816.

Subgenus *Janthina* s.s.

Common Purple Sea Snail
Janthina (Janthina) janthina (Linné, 1758)

Pale Purple Sea Snail
Janthina (Janthina) pallida (Thompson, 1841)

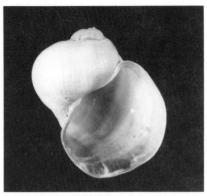

Size: 32 mm.
Color: Purple on basal part of shell, lavender or white above (floats with purple side up).
Shape: Low conic; body whorl very large and gently angular.
Ornament or sculpture: Smooth, very fragile.
Aperture: More or less subquadrate with columellar edge almost vertical; outer lip very delicate, lower edge horizontal.
Habitat: Pelagic in warm seas.
Localities: Entire.
Occurrence: Seasonally common.
Range: Pelagic in most warm seas.
Remarks: Foot builds float by trapping air bubbles in mucus; exudes purple stain when disturbed; carnivorous, feeding on Portuguese men-of-war, *Velella*, and other violet-colored coelenterates; strong southeast wind in spring will literally cover beach with them, next year might not appear at all; beware of Portuguese men-of-war that wash in with them.

Size: 12–18 mm.
Color: Purplish white with pale lavender on early whorls and along margin of outer lip.
Shape: Globose conic.
Ornament or sculpture: Appears smooth but has fine, irregular axial growth lines; body whorl large, rounded, swollen.
Aperture: Subquadrate, somewhat flaring at base; thin outer margin of lip slightly sinuate near center where float attached; interior violet along columella and base, fainter over remainder.
Habitat: Pelagic in warm seas.
Localities: Entire.
Occurrence: Uncommon, seasonal.
Range: Pelagic in most warm seas.
Remarks: Easily confused with *J. prolongata*, only recently recognized as occurring in this area; attaches eggs to bottom of float.

Subgenus *Violetta* Iredale, 1929

Globe Purple Sea Snail
Janthina (Violetta) prolongata
  Blainville, 1822

Size: 12–18 mm.
Color: Deep violet throughout.
Shape: Globose with low spire; body
whorl very large.
Ornament or sculpture: Smooth, very
fragile; very fine growth lines.
Aperture: Subquadrate, very large;
columella vertical; outer lip has sinuous
margin; indentation marks point of
attachment of float.
Habitat: Pelagic in warm seas.
Localities: Entire.
Occurrence: Fairly common.
Range: Pelagic in warm waters; both
coasts of United States.
Remarks: Syn. *J. globosa* (Swainson,
1823) [not Blainville, 1822]; attaches
eggs to float; less numerous and more
delicate than *J. janthina*; remove
animals by "watering out" (see
Cleaning).

Genus *Recluzia* Petit de la Saussaye,
  1853

Brown Sea Snail
Recluzia rollaniana Petit, 1853 [See
  SST, p. 115]

Superfamily EULIMACEA Risso, 1826
Family EULIMIDAE Risso, 1826

Genus *Niso* Risso, 1826

Niso aegless Bush, 1885 [See *SST*,
  p. 116]

Genus *Eulima* Risso, 1826 =
  [*Strombiformis* of authors, not
  Da Costa, 1778]

Two-Lined Melanella
Eulima cf. *E. bilineatus* (Alder, 1848)

Size: 8 mm.
Color: Whitish with 2 brownish lines
on each whorl; polished.
Shape: Elongate conic, very slender.
Ornament or sculpture: 10 flattened
whorls, sutures fairly distinct; gradually
tapers to sharp apex that may be
deflected.
Aperture: Elongated pyriform; entire;
outer lip sharp; columella concave.
Habitat: Thought to be ectoparasitic on
holothurians in shallow waters;
epifaunal.
Localities: Entire.
Occurrence: Uncommon in beach drift.
Range: Europe; North Carolina to
West Indies; Texas; Brazil.
Remarks: [*Strombiformis bilineata*].
Syn. *S. bifaciatus*.

Genus *Melanella* Bowdich, 1822

Curved Melanella
Melanella arcuanta C.B. Adams, 1850

Size: 4 mm.
Color: Glossy white.
Shape: Ovate conic.
Ornament or sculpture: 10 convex whorls with lightly impressed suture; fine impressed spiral line above suture marks smooth shell; spire with axis curved to extraordinary degree in upper whorls.
Aperture: Rather long ovate.
Habitat: Ectoparasitic on sea cucumbers; epifaunal.
Localities: Central and south.
Occurrence: Uncommon in beach drift.
Range: North Carolina; Texas; West Indies.
Remarks: Type specimen lost. [*Balcis arcuata*].

Genus *Polygireulima* Sacco, 1892

Jamaica Melanella
Polygireulima jamaicensis (C.B. Adams, 1845)

Size: 6–12 mm.
Color: Glossy white.
Shape: Elongate conic.
Ornament or sculpture: 12 to 14 flat-sided whorls; polished whorls taper to slightly bent sharp apex; sutures not well defined; anomphalous.
Aperture: Pyriform, slender; outer lip thin but slightly thickened at base; columella concave.
Habitat: Ectoparasitic; bays; epifaunal.
Localities: Entire.
Occurrence: Fairly common in beach drift.
Range: Florida; Texas; Carmen, Campeche, Mexico; Gulf of Campeche; Costa Rica[?]; West Indies.
Remarks: May be *Melanella intermedia* Contraine, 1835; has been referred to as *Balcis conoidea* Kurtz & Stimpson, 1851, but lacks distinct basal ridge and rhomboidal aperture of that species. Syn. *P. intermedia* Contraine. [*Balcis jamaicensis* C.B. Adams]

Family ACLIDIDAE G.O. Sars, 1878

Genus *Graphis* Jeffreys, 1867

Graphis underwoodae Bartsch, 1947
[See *SST*, p. 118]

Genus *Henrya* Bartsch, 1947

Henrya goldmani Bartsch, 1947 [See *SST*, p. 118]

Superfamily STROMBACEA
Rafinesque, 1815
Family STROMBIDAE Rafinesque,
1815

Genus *Strombus* Linné, 1758

Fighting Conch
Strombus alatus Gmelin, 1791

Size: 75–100 mm.
Color: Dark reddish brown to lighter brown; some mottled or with zigzag markings.
Shape: Conic.
Ornament or sculpture: Spire has 8 whorls; body whorl is four-fifths of total length of heavy, solid shell; wide shoulders with or without short spines; spiral striations near base; sutures distinct; anomphalous.
Aperture: Long, narrow; lip has broad outward flare; interior polished;

somewhat flared siphonal notch at base and rounded notch in lip just above it.
Habitat: Intertidal to about 18 meters (10 fathoms); epifaunal.
Localities: Entire.
Occurrence: Uncommon beach shell.
Range: South Carolina; both sides of Florida; Texas.
Remarks: This grazing scavenger has well-developed eyes on long eye stalks on head; long, narrow foot tipped with clawlike operculum moves animal about in awkward leaps; can right itself and return to water if beached by wave; Hurricane Carla (1961) stranded thousands on southern half of Padre Island; eggs laid in gelatinous ribbons.

Superfamily CALYPTRAEACEA
Blainville, 1824
Family CALYPTRAEIDAE Blainville,
1824
Subfamily CREPIDULINAE Fleming,
1799

Genus *Crepidula* Lamarck, 1799
Subgenus *Crepidula* s.s.

Faded Slipper Shell
Crepidula (Crepidula) convexa Say,
1822

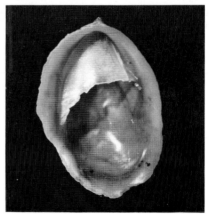

Size: Length 12 mm, width 8 mm.
Color: Translucent tan or mottled with reddish brown; internal septum white.
Shape: Limpetlike, low, oval with apex near margin; varies corresponding to shape of attachment site.
Ornament or sculpture: Smooth with centrally located apex.
Aperture: Very large oval with thin margin; internal deck, or septum, deep-seated, convex, supports soft parts.
Habitat: Intertidal to moderate depths on shell, rocks, grass; epifaunal.
Localities: Entire.
Occurrence: Common.
Range: Bermuda; Massachusetts to Florida; Texas; Yucatán; Quintana Roo; West Indies; California.
Remarks: Commensal with living *Argopecten irradians amplicostatus* and some gastropods, preferring to be near outer lip of host.

Aperture: Oval, oblique, with thin margin; polished interior; deck occupies about half of aperture; white margin sinuous.
Habitat: 1 to 8 meters (6 fathoms); epifaunal on exoskeleton.
Localities: Entire.
Occurrence: Common.
Range: Canada to Florida and Texas; Yucatán; introduced to California and England.
Remarks: Adult shell sedentary and tends to pile up in stacks of up to 19 individuals that gradually diminish in size; frequently on olive shells; stack of protandric mollusks will have right margin of each member in contact with right margin of one it is on; bottom and larger animals are female, top are males, and those in between are in transitional stages; eggs brooded in mantle cavity.

Common Atlantic Slipper Shell
Crepidula (Crepidula) fornicata (Linné, 1758)

Subgenus *Ianacus* Mörch, 1852
Eastern White Slipper Shell
Crepidula (Ianacus) plana Say, 1822

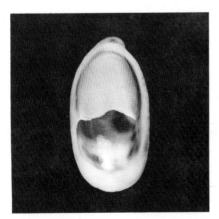

Size: 51 mm.
Color: Dirty white to tan with mottlings of brown shades.
Shape: Limpetlike, oval oblique; curved to fit place of attachment.
Ornament or sculpture: Smooth except for fine growth lines; body whorl major part of shell; apex turned to one side.

Size: Length up to 30 mm.
Color: White.
Shape: Elongate oval, flat; conforms to attachment site.
Ornament or sculpture: Smooth except for fine growth lines; apex depressed.

Aperture: Large, oval with thin margin; deck about half length of shell, notched to one side; polished.
Habitat: Intertidal to moderate depths; epifaunal.
Localities: Entire.
Occurrence: Common.
Range: Bermuda; Canada to Florida; Gulf states; Texas; Gulf of Mexico to Quintana Roo; rare in West Indies; Surinam; Brazil.
Remarks: Not as particular as to attachment site as *C. fornicata* and *C. convexa*—dead shell, old bottles, piers, oysters, tires, all will do; as a result shape of this flat shell can be quite varied; eggs brooded under shell.

Superfamily LAMELLARIACEA Orbigny, 1841
Family LAMELLARIIDAE Orbigny 1841 = [VELUTINIDAE Gray, 1840]
Subfamily LAMELLARIINAE Orbigny, 1841

Genus *Lamellaria* Montagu, 1815
Rang's Lamellaria
Lamellaria cf. *L. leucosphaera* Schwengel, 1942 [See *SST*, p. 121]

Superfamily TRIVIACEA Gray, 1852
Family TRIVIIDAE Gray, 1852
Subfamily TRIVIINAE Troschel, 1863

Genus *Trivia* Gray, 1852
Subgenus *Pusula* Jousseaume, 1884
Suffuse Trivia
Trivia (Pusula) suffusa (Gray, 1832) [See *SST*, p. 122]

Superfamily CYPRAEACEA Rafinesque, 1815
Family CYPRAEIDAE Rafinesque, 1815
Subfamily CYPRAEINAE Rafinesque, 1815

Genus *Cypraea* Linné, 1758
Subgenus *Macrocypraea* Schilder, 1930

Atlantic Deer Cowrie
Cypraea (Macrocypraea) cervus Linné, 1771

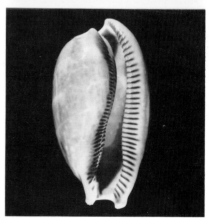

Size: 75–125 mm.
Color: Polished light brown, with large, round, white spots on dorsal side; whitish dorsal line.
Shape: Elongate oval; spire concealed.

Ornament or sculpture: Smooth, polished.
Aperture: Long, narrow; outer lip rolled inward, brownish without spots; edge outlined with regular, small, alternating brown and white riblets; similar but less distinct riblets on inner lip; purplish interior.
Habitat: Offshore reefs; epifaunal.
Localities: Port Aransas, south.
Occurrence: Uncommon beach shell.
Range: Southeastern Florida to Yucatán; Brazil.
Remarks: Pinkish brown and whitish mantle covered with short papillae and envelops entire shell; at rest, shell is covered, but when touched, animal draws into shell; female lays eggs in gelatinous mass of 500 to 1,500 capsules, which she broods; this carnivore grazes on algae and colonial invertebrates; nocturnal; beach shells have smooth worn place on underside parallel to aperture.

Family OVULIDAE Gray, 1853

Genus *Simnialena* Cate, 1973

Sea Whip Simnia
Simnialena marferula Cate, 1973

Size: 8.4 mm.
Color: Orange yellow to medium rose, glossy.

Shape: Elongate, tapering at both ends.
Ornament or sculpture: Smooth, with numerous irregularly incised, transverse lines covering entire dorsal area; base finely transversely striate throughout.
Aperture: Broad, widening even more to front; outer lip fairly heavily, roundly calloused; outer surface uneven, subcrenulate.
Habitat: On sea whip coral, *Leptogorgia setacea*; epifaunal.
Localities: Entire.
Occurrence: Common in beach drift.
Range: Texas coast.
Remarks: Cate (in litt.) says this has been called *Neosimnia uniplicata* (Sowerby II, 1848), a long slender form without dorsal striation but striated at each end of shell.

Single-Toothed Simnia
Simnialena uniplicata (G. B. Sowerby II, 1848)

Size: 20.2 mm.
Color: Deep rose brown overall, except that outer lip, front base, adaxial carina, and portions of rear terminal beak white.
Shape: Long, narrow, subcylindrical; ends tapering.
Ornament or sculpture: Smooth, glossy except for incised striae restricted to either end.

Aperture: Broad, flaring toward front; outer lip thinly, roundly thickened, with weak callus shouldering above.
Habitat: On soft coral, *Eugorgia virgulata*; epifaunal.
Localities: Port Aransas, south.
Occurrence: Uncommon in beach drift.
Range: Virginia to both coasts of Florida; possibly Honduras and east coast of Central America.
Remarks: Previously misidentified (J. Andrews 1971, p. 98) as *Neosimnia acicularis* (Lamarck, 1810), which is *Cymbula acicularis*.

Genus *Pseudocyphoma* Cate, 1973

Weak-Ridge Cyphoma
Pseudocyphoma intermedium
  (G. B. Sowerby I, 1828)

Size: 30 mm.
Color: White, glossy.
Shape: Shell ovate oblong (diamond-shaped), somewhat acuminated at both ends, more so at upper than at lower.
Ornament or sculpture: Back with transverse, raised rounded angle rather above middle; smooth, semi-glossy, except for fine transverse striae above either end.
Aperture: Narrow at upper end, broader at lower; columellar lip with single oblique plait; outer lip thickened; inner edge smooth, without teeth.
Habitat: On soft corals; epifaunal.
Localities: Port Aransas; Port Isabel.
Occurrence: Rare.

Range: Texas; Dominican Republic; West Indies; Surinam.
Remarks: Figured twice and identified as *Cyphoma intermedium* and misidentified as *C. mcgintyi* (Pilsbry, 1939) in J. Andrews (1971, pp. 98–99). Following killing freeze of January 1962 live specimens washed in; colorful, maculated animal, which envelops shell; spoil-bank specimens less humped.

Superfamily NATICACEA (Swainson), Gray, 1840
Family NATICIDAE (Swainson), Gray, 1840
Subfamily POLINICINAE Gray, 1847

Genus *Polinices* Montfort, 1810
Subgenus *Neverita* Risso, 1826

Shark's Eye
Polinices (Neverita) duplicatus (Say, 1822)

Size: Diameter 26–37 mm.
Color: Porcelaneous, glossy, gray to tan, often strikingly marked with orange brown; underside whitish; callus in bay specimens often rich purple.
Shape: Globose, low spire, expanded body whorl; bay specimens have higher spires than Gulf ones.
Ornament or sculpture: Smooth with fine growth lines.
Aperture: Large, subcircular; outer lip thin; columella oblique; umbilicus deep, partly closed by heavy callus; no siphonal canal.
Habitat: Shallow waters of both bay and Gulf; infaunal.
Localities: Entire.
Occurrence: Common.
Range: Cape Cod to Florida and Gulf states.
Remarks: Plows through sand in search of bivalves and snails; wraps foot about prey, begins slow process of drilling round hole in shell, inserting proboscis, and rasping out soft parts with radula, often tiring before completion; does not feed unless buried; female builds collar of mucus and sand over margin of aperture when spawning. The bay form is darker, rounder, and more elevated than those offshore.

Subgenus *Polinices* s.s.

Brown Moon Shell
Polinices (Polinices) hepaticus (Röding, 1798) [See *SST*, p. 125]

Subfamily NATICINAE Swainson, 1840

Genus *Natica* Scopoli, 1777
Subgenus *Naticarius* Dumeril, 1806

Colorful Atlantic Natica
Natica (Naticarius) canrena (Linné, 1758) [See *SST*, p. 126]

Subgenus *Tectonatica* Sacco, 1890

Miniature Natica
Natica (Tectonatica) pusilla Say, 1822

Size: Diameter 6–8 mm.
Color: White to fawn brown, faint reddish brown markings.
Shape: Subglobular; spire depressed, body whorl expanded.
Ornament or sculpture: Smooth with fine growth lines, porcelaneous.
Aperture: Large, semilunar; outer lip thin; columella oblique; callus strong, practically covering umbilicus, but often has small opening next to umbilical callus.
Habitat: Shallow inlet areas; infaunal.
Localities: Entire.
Occurrence: Fairly common.
Range: Eastern United States; Gulf states; Carmen, Campeche, Mexico; Gulf of Campeche; West Indies; Surinam; northeastern Brazil.
Remarks: Corneous operculum distinguishes it from similar appearance of juvenile *Polinices duplicatus*.

Subfamily SININAE Woodring, 1928

Genus *Sinum* Röding, 1798

Maculated Baby's Ear
Sinum maculatum (Say, 1831) [See *SST*, p. 127]

Common Baby's Ear
Sinum perspectivum (Say, 1831)

Range: Bermuda; southeastern United States; Gulf states; Campeche Bank; West Indies; Surinam; Brazil.
Remarks: Animal almost completely envelops shell; exudes surprising quantity of clear mucus when touched; at low tide, fed on by racoons.

Superfamily TONNACEA Suter, 1913
Family CASSIDAE Latreille, 1825

Genus *Phalium* Link, 1807
Subgenus *Tylocassis* Woodring, 1928

Scotch Bonnet
Phalium (Tylocassis) granulatum granulatum (Born, 1780)

Size: Diameter 25−51 mm.
Color: White.
Shape: Auriform, greatly flattened; apex on same plane as body whorl.
Ornament or sculpture: About 3 whorls; sutures slightly impressed; many fine spiral growth lines on top of whorls.
Aperture: Large, rounded; outer lip sharp; columella curved.
Habitat: Along outer beaches and inlet areas in sand; infaunal.
Localities: Entire.
Occurrence: Common.

Size: Length 25–100 mm.
Color: Background white or cream with spiral bands of regularly spaced yellowish brown squares.
Shape: Oval with slightly extended spire.
Ornament or sculpture: Body whorl about three-fourths of shell length; some specimens have small nodules on shoulder edge; deeply grooved spirally, raised spiral cords slightly convex and wider than spaces between them; transverse sculpture of fine lines gives overall reticulated pattern.
Aperture: Semilunar, length of body whorl; outer lip thickened, reflexed with regular, small teeth on both edges; interior fawn colored; parietal wall glazed, smooth with lower area pustulose; short siphonal canal upturned to left.
Habitat: Just offshore in warm seas; epifaunal.
Localities: Entire, more to south.
Occurrence: Fairly common.
Range: Bermuda; North Carolina to Gulf states; West Indies; Surinam; Brazil.
Remarks: Mantle cream colored with close dark spots; predatory on sand dollars and sea urchins; eggs laid in tower of horny capsules.

Genus *Cypraecassis* Stutchbury, 1837

Reticulated Cowrie Helmet
Cypraecassis testiculus (Linné, 1758)
[See *SST*, p. 129]

Family TONNIDAE Suter, 1913

Genus *Tonna* Brunnich, 1772

Giant Tun Shell
Tonna galea (Linné, 1758)

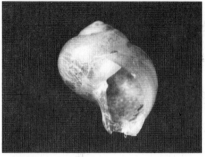

(juvenile)

Size: Up to 160 mm.
Color: Creamy white to light coffee brown, generally uniform.
Shape: Globose; spire slightly extended, thin.
Ornament or sculpture: 7 to 7½ very convex whorls; body whorl dominates shell; suture deep, channeled; spiral sculpture consists of 19 to 21 rather broad, flattened ridges; usually finer ridge between 2 of larger ones on upper half of whorl; fine axial growth lines; umbilicate.
Aperture: Subovate, large; outer lip thin, crenulate until maturity; at

maturity becomes reflexed and develops thickened ridge well below lip margin; parietal area glazed; columella short, twisted with ridge along outer edge that ends at siphonal canal.
Habitat: Near-shore sandy bottoms and inlet areas; epifaunal.
Localities: Entire.
Occurrence: Uncommon to rare; rarely taken alive in vicinity of Aransas ship channel.
Range: North Carolina to Florida; Gulf states; Campeche Bank; West Indies; Surinam; Brazil; Indo-Pacific; Mediterranean.
Remarks: Free-swimming, pelagic young may be found in spring in beach drift; embryonic shells smooth, golden brown in color, and somewhat pliable; 3 to 4 whorls; aperture closed with tightly fitting operculum; in winter months on upper Mexican Gulf beaches, drift will be lined with young tuns about size of egg; animal has large foot and long proboscis, is yellowish in color and heavily mottled with black.

Superfamily CYMATIACEA ?Iredale, 1913
Family CYMATIIDAE Iredale, 1913

Genus *Cymatium* Röding, 1798
Subgenus *Gutturnium* Mörch, 1852

Knobbed Triton
Cymatium (Gutturnium) muricinum
(Röding, 1798) [See *SST*, p. 130]

Subgenus *Cymatriton* Clench & Turner, 1957

Gold-Mouthed Triton
Cymatium (Cymatriton) nicobaricum
(Röding, 1798) [See *SST*, p. 131]

Subgenus *Septa* Perry, 1810

Atlantic Hairy Triton
Cymatium (Septa) pileare (Linné, 1758)
[See *SST*, p. 132]

Subgenus *Linatella* Gray, 1857

Poulsen's Triton
Cymatium (Linatella) cingulatum
(Lamarck, 1822)

Size: 31–62 mm.
Color: Light brown to straw yellow, occasionally banded with brown.
Shape: Globose conic with extended siphonal canal.
Ornament or sculpture: 4 post-embryonic whorls; convex; body whorl slightly shouldered; suture slightly indented; spiral sculpture consists of 18 to 20 flattened cords with fine threads in between; shoulder cord might be slightly beaded; transverse sculpture of fine growth lines, some with thin, bladelike varix; anomphalous.
Aperture: Subelliptical; outer lip crenulated, slightly expanded; parietal area glazed; columella arched inward, continuing as margin of siphonal canal; canal variable, moderately long, upturned.
Habitat: Offshore to 411 meters (209 fathoms); epifaunal.
Localities: Central, south.
Occurrence: Uncommon to rare.
Range: Bermuda; North Carolina; Florida south to West Indies to

Venezuela; Texas; Mexico; Surinam; southern Brazil.

Remarks: Shell said to be rare, but at times can be picked up by bushelfuls along Mexican coast just south of Rio Grande; syn. *C. poulsenii* Mörch, 1877.

Subgenus *Monoplex* Perry, 1811

Von Salis' Triton
Cymatium (Monoplex) parthenopeum
  (Von Salis, 1793)

Size: Up to 90 mm.
Color: Usually light brownish yellow; may have spiral bands of slightly darker brown becoming darker on varices.
Shape: Conic with extended siphonal canal.
Ornament or sculpture: 7 to 8 postembryonic whorls, convex, shouldered; spire moderately extended; suture slightly indented; spiral sculpture consists of 5 or 6 broad, low, often nodulose cords, with many finer threads in interspaces and on cords; transverse sculpture of fine growth lines with 2 low varices in adults.
Aperture: Subelliptical; outer lip bordered with paired teeth opposite grooves between external spiral cords; parietal wall dark reddish brown with numerous, irregular, white plications; anal canal bordered with ridge on parietal wall; short siphon, upturned,

with columella extending into it at parietal margin.
Habitat: Below low water to 63 meters (35 fathoms); epifaunal.
Localities: Extreme south.
Occurrence: Uncommon to rare.
Range: Bermuda; North Carolina; Florida; Texas; Mexico; West Indies; Surinam south to Brazil; Uruguay; Indo-Pacific; Japan.
Remarks: Syn. *C. costatum* Born, 1778; more often found on beach south of Rio Grande; found on both sides of Panama.

Genus *Distorsio* Röding, 1798
Subgenus *Rhysema* Clench & Turner, 1957

Atlantic Distorsio
Distorsio (Rhysema) clathrata
  (Lamarck, 1816)

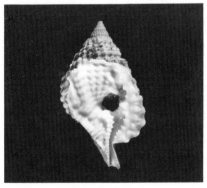

Size: 25–75 mm.
Color: Grayish white.
Shape: Conic with siphonal canal.
Ornament or sculpture: 10 irregular, convex whorls; spire extended; suture slightly impressed, irregular; spiral sculpture consists of numerous low cords interspaced with fine spiral threads; transverse sculpture of numerous cords that cross spiral cords, producing reticulated pattern with small knobs at point of crossing; 7 to 9 varices.

Aperture: Auriculate with thickened outer lip; outer lip has 10 denticles, third below anal canal largest and opposite deep parietal embayment; inner lip has numerous plicae; 2 large parietal plicae border posterior canal; spiral cords thickened in parietal embayment, continuing as plicae on columella, which is nearly straight and upturned; wide, thinly glazed parietal shield bordered by thin varix ridge.
Habitat: Just below low water to 54 meters (30 fathoms) in warm seas; epifaunal.
Localities: Entire.
Occurrence: Uncommon.
Range: Southeastern United States; Gulf states; Campeche Bank; Caribbean; Surinam; Brazil.
Remarks: Distorted aperture basis for name.

Suborder SIPHONOSTOMATA Blainville, 1824 = [STENOGLOSSA Troschel, 1848, and NEOGASTROPODA Thiele, 1925]
Superfamily CANCELLARIACEA Gray, 1853
Family CANCELLARIIDAE Forbes & Hanley, 1853

Genus *Cancellaria* Lamarck, 1799

Common Nutmeg
Cancellaria reticulata (Linné, 1767) [See *SST*, p. 135]

Superfamily CONACEA Rafinesque, 1815
Family TURRIDAE H. & A. Adams, 1853
Subfamily CRASSISPIRINAE

Genus *Crassispira* Swainson, 1840
Subgenus *Crassispirella* Bartsch & Rehder, 1939

Oyster Turret
Crassispira (Crassispirella) tampaensis Bartsch & Rehder, 1939 [See *SST*, p. 135]

Subfamily MANGELIINAE Fischer, 1883

Genus *Kurtziella* Dall, 1918
Subgenus *Kurtziella* s.s.

Brown-Tipped Mangelia
Kurtziella (Kurtziella) cf. *K. atrostyla* (Tryon, 1884) [See *SST*, p. 136]

Waxen Mangelia
Kurtziella (Kurtziella) cf. *K. cerina* (Kurtz & Stimpson, 1851)

Size: 9 mm.
Color: Waxen white to ash color on upper whorls; no lines of color.
Shape: Turriculate.
Ornament or sculpture: Spire equal to last whorl; 5 postnuclear whorls, flattish, angulated on shoulder; small larval whorls, smooth except for last, which has 4 nodulous spiral lines; granulous spiral sculpture; 9 swollen transverse riblets; no varix; suture adpressed, undulated.
Aperture: Narrow, oblique, about one-half length of body whorl; notch well marked, away from suture; canal very short.
Habitat: Mud flats between tides; hypersaline lagoons and inlet areas; epifaunal[?].
Localities: Entire.
Occurrence: Fairly common in beach drift.
Range: Massachusetts; North Carolina; both sides of Florida; Texas.

Remarks: Specimens usually worn and difficult to identify; [*Mangelia cerina*].

Punctate Mangelia
Kurtziella (Kurtziella) cf. *K. limonitella* (Dall, 1884)

Size: 9 mm.
Color: Whitish, lineated spirally with yellow brown; some brown on outside of canal.
Shape: Turriculate.
Ornament or sculpture: Spire trifle shorter than last whorl; 5 postnuclear whorls, rounded angulated behind periphery; spiral sculpture granulose; 12 narrow, transverse riblets; no varix; ribs obsolete on fasciole; suture hardly adpressed or undulated.
Aperture: Narrow, oblique; notch shallow, deepest at angulation; canal not distinct from aperture.
Habitat: Offshore banks and mud flats between tides; hypersaline lagoons and inlets; epifaunal[?].
Localities: Entire.
Occurrence: Fairly common.
Range: North Carolina to both sides of Florida; Texas.
Remarks: Does not have little beads on last nuclear whorl that *K. cerina* has; [*Drillia limonitella*], [*Mangelia limonitella*]. [Figured specimen in *SST*, p. 137, is *Cryoturris* cf. *C. Cerinella* (Dall, 1889)].

Subgenus *Rubellatoma* Bartsch & Rehder, 1939

Reddish Mangelia
Kurtziella (Rubellatoma) cf. *K. rubella* (Kurtz & Stimpson, 1851) [See *SST*, p. 138]

Genus *Cryoturris* Woodring, 1828

Wax-Colored Mangelia
Cryoturris cf. *C. cerinella* (Dall, 1889)

Size: 10.5 mm.
Color: Whitish toward apex, ashy on intermediate, orangish on body whorl; never striped or spotted.
Shape: Turriculate, drawn out, slender.
Ornament or sculpture: 7 postnuclear whorls, angulate at periphery and sloping either way from it; granulose spiral sculpture; 6 or 7 transverse ribs; suture less adpressed and undulated than *Kurtziella cerina*.
Aperture: Long, narrow, oblique; hardly any indentation for notch; no canal to speak of.
Habitat: Mud flats between tides; hypersaline lagoons and inlets; epifaunal[?].
Localities: Entire.
Occurrence: Fairly common in beach drift.
Range: North Carolina to both sides of Florida; Texas.
Remarks: Beach specimens very worn; [*Kurtziella cerinella*].

Genus *Nannodiella* Dall, 1919

Nannodiella cf. *N. vespuciana*
  (Orbigny, 1842)

Size: 5 mm.
Color: Yellowish white, tinged with brown just below suture and on anterior part of body whorl.
Shape: Fusiform.
Ornament or sculpture: 8 postnuclear whorls strongly angulated just below middle, ornamented with about 9 rather prominent, straight transverse ribs, commencing at periphery and extending to suture; these, with their wide, concave interspaces, are crossed by 3 strong, rounded, equally distant threads, the third defining suture; where these cross ribs, nodules are formed; nucleus smooth, glassy; surface granulose.
Aperture: Narrow ovate, pinched up anteriorly into short, rather narrow, straight canal; outer lip thickened, with conspicuous varix and thick, smooth, rounded, irregularly curved, light brown edge; deep, narrow sinus considerably below suture, at angle of shoulder; columella slightly curved.
Habitat: Probably offshore; epifaunal[?].
Localities: East, central.
Occurrence: Uncommon in beach drift.

Range: North Carolina; Gulf states.
Remarks: Syn. *Mangelia oxytata* Bush, 1885.

Genus *Pyrgocythara* Woodring, 1928

Plicate Mangelia
Pyrgocythara plicosa (C. B. Adams, 1850)

Size: 6–8 mm.
Color: Reddish brown; dead shells wax colored.
Shape: Turriculate; spire about one-half length.
Ornament or sculpture: 6 to 7 whorls; sutures distinct; only slightly shouldered; spiral sculpture of strong, regularly spaced cords; 11 to 12 transverse ribs made nodulose by spiral cords.
Aperture: Semilunar; outer lip thickened with very pronounced posterior notch below suture; interior dark; parietal lip narrow; siphonal canal short.
Habitat: Shallow, hypersaline lagoon on grass or mud bottom; epifaunal[?].
Localities: Entire.
Occurrence: Common.
Range: Cape Cod to western Florida; Texas.
Remarks: Posterior notch eases identification; [*Mangelia plicosa*].

Family TEREBRIDAE Mörch, 1852

Genus *Terebra* Bruguière, 1792

Common Atlantic Auger
Terebra dislocata (Say, 1822)

Flame Auger
Terebra taurinus (Lightfoot, 1986)

Size: 37–51 mm.
Color: Grayish white to orangish white.
Shape: Turriculate.
Ornament or sculpture: Numerous slightly convex whorls with about 15 axial ribs per whorl; sutures distinct with beaded spiral band just below and fine spiral striae between ribs.
Aperture: Small, subovate; outer lip thin with recurved siphonal notch at base; columella short; narrow parietal area polished.
Habitat: Inlet areas; infaunal.
Localities: Entire.
Occurrence: Common.
Range: Maryland to Florida; Texas; West Indies; Brazil.
Remarks: Can be found under bulges of sand at low tides.

Size: 100–150 mm.
Color: Background cream with axial reddish brown, flame-shaped marks in two spiral rows.
Shape: Turriculate, slender.
Ornament or sculpture: About 14 flattened whorls; sutures distinct; 2 spiral incised lines between sutures; numerous fine, wavy transverse striations.
Aperture: Semilunar, oblique, short; thin outer lip; columella convexly curved; anterior or siphonal canal short, recurved.
Habitat: Deeper water offshore; infaunal.
Localities: Central, south.
Occurrence: Uncommon to rare.
Range: Southeastern Florida; Gulf of Mexico; West Indies; Surinam; Brazil.
Remarks: Usually takes hurricane to bring in greatly prized broken shells; syn. *T. flammea* Lamarck, 1822.

Subgenus *Strioterebrum* Sacco, 1891
Fine-Ribbed Auger
Terebra (Strioterebrum) protexta
(Conrad, 1846)

Genus *Hastula* H. & A. Adams, 1853
Marylee's Terebra
Hastula maryleeae R. D. Burch, 1965

Size: 20–25 mm.
Color: Brownish when living.
Shape: Turriculate.
Ornament or sculpture: 13 to 15 slightly convex whorls; suture distinct; spiral sculpture of band below suture similar to but less pronounced than *T. dislocata*; convex, axial riblets crossed by fine spiral striations.
Aperture: Small, oblique, oval; outer lip thin; parietal area narrow, glossy; columella short with upturned siphonal notch at base.
Habitat: Offshore in 1.8–90 meters (1–50 fathoms); inlet areas; infaunal.
Localities: Entire.
Occurrence: Fairly common.
Range: North Carolina to Florida; Texas; Campeche Bank; Yucatán; Caribbean; Brazil.
Remarks: Alive at San Luis Pass.

Size: 25–51 mm.
Color: Variable from ivory white to dark purplish gray; polished.
Shape: Elongate conic.
Ornament or sculpture: Numerous flat-sided whorls; sutures distinct; apex very pointed; numerous small axial riblets near suture; spiral sculpture of microstriations; rows of punctations typical of *Hastula* absent.
Aperture: Small, pear-shaped; outer lip thin, with deep, recurved siphonal notch at base.
Habitat: Sandy surf zone; infaunal.
Localities: Entire, more to south.
Occurrence: Common.
Range: From Galveston, Texas, to Veracruz, Mexico; Yucatán.
Remarks: Holotype collected at Surfside beach, Freeport, Texas, by Marylee Burch on March 16, 1961.

Sallé's Auger
Hastula salleana Deshayes, 1859

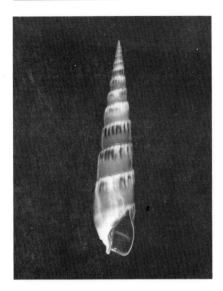

Size: 25–51 mm.
Color: Dark bluish gray or brownish; polished.
Shape: Elongate conic.
Ornament or sculpture: Numerous flat-sided whorls; sutures distinct; apex very pointed; about 30 short, dark ribs below suture of each whorl; spiral sculpture of microscopic rows of punctations, more widely spaced than in *H. cinera* Born, 1780.
Aperture: Small, pear-shaped, dark brown within; outer lip thin, with deep siphonal notch at base; sharp ridge runs from notch to mid-columella.
Habitat: Sandy surf zone; infaunal.
Localities: Entire, more to south.
Occurrence: Common.
Range: Florida west to Veracruz, Mexico; Colombia; Brazil.
Remarks: During warm months in surf zone with *H. maryleeae* Burch and *Donax* clams; fed on by starfish, *Luida clathrata*; [*Terebra salleana*]; has been listed as *T. cinerea* Born, 1780.

Family BUCCINIDAE Rafinesque, 1815

Genus *Cantharus* Röding, 1789

Cancellate Cantharus
Cantharus cancellarius (Conrad, 1846)

Size: 18–28 mm.
Color: Yellowish brown.
Shape: Ovate conic.
Ornament or sculpture: 5 to 6 convex, heavy whorls; spire conical; spiral sculpture of sharp cords that form beads and cross narrow transverse ribs, making reticulate pattern.
Aperture: Long oval, glossy white; outer lip thin, crenulate with fine denticulations on inner edge; posterior canal weak or absent; siphonal canal straight, short, slightly upturned; one plica at base of columella.
Habitat: Shallow water in rocky places, inlet areas; epifaunal.
Localities: Entire.
Occurrence: Common seasonally.
Range: Western coast of Florida to Texas; Yucatán.
Remarks: Lives on jetties.

Genus *Pisania* Bivona, 1832

Tinted Cantharus
Pisania tincta (Conrad, 1846)

Family NASSARIIDAE Iredale, 1916.

Genus *Nassarius* Dumeril, 1806
Subgenus *Nassarius* s.s.

Sharp-Knobbed Nassa
Nassarius (Nassarius) acutus (Say, 1822)

Size: 18–28 mm.
Color: Variable: blue gray, yellow, chocolate, milk white; darkest at apex.
Shape: Ovate conic.
Ornament or sculpture: 5 to 6 convex, heavy whorls; spire conical; spiral sculpture of cords with finer threads in between, crossing over weak axial ribs; weak nodules on whorl shoulder.
Aperture: Oval; outer lip thickened, denticulate on inner edge; parietal lip glazed; plica on upper part borders small posterior or abaxial canal; siphonal canal almost straight, slightly upturned.
Habitat: Shallow water, rocks, seaweed close to shore; epifaunal.
Localities: Port Aransas, south.
Occurrence: Fairly common.
Range: North Carolina to both sides of Florida; Texas; Campeche Bank; West Indies; eastern Brazil.
Remarks: Alive on jetties; dead in rolls of sea whip coral; [*Cantharus tinctus*].

Size: 6–12 mm.
Color: Cream white to yellowish, occasionally with brown spiral thread.
Shape: Ovate conic.
Ornament or sculpture: 7 convex whorls; spire pointed and longer than body whorl; spiral sculpture of spiral threads that cross similar transverse ribs, giving beaded, cancellate appearance to shell.
Aperture: Oval, slightly oblique; short recurved siphonal canal.
Habitat: Open lagoon, inlet, along shore; semi-infaunal.
Localities: Entire.
Occurrence: Common.
Range: Western coast of Florida to Texas.
Remarks: This scavenger attracted by smell of decaying flesh and by light; feeds on debris, other mollusks, and mollusk egg capsules; lays eggs in gelatinous capsules attached to bottom; young *Anadara brasiliana* attach with byssus to shell of *N. acutus* in symbiotic relationship.

Common Eastern Nassa
Nassarius (Nassarius) vibex (Say, 1822)

Family FASCIOLARIIDAE Gray, 1853
Subfamily FASCIOLARIINAE Gray, 1853

Genus *Fasciolaria* Lamarck, 1799
Subgenus *Fasciolaria* s.s.

Banded Tulip Shell
Fasciolaria (Fasciolaria) lilium
Fischer von Waldheim, 1807

Size: 12 mm.
Color: Gray brown to whitish with a few splotches of darker brown.
Shape: Ovate conic.
Ornament or sculpture: 7 convex whorls; body whorl dominates short, heavy shell; spiral sculpture of fine threads that cross about 12 transverse ribs; sutures shallow; apex acute.
Aperture: Oval, small; outer lip with thick varix, denticulate within; columella arched, short; parietal area well developed, glazed white; siphonal canal short, slightly upturned.
Habitat: In bay and open-sound margins and inlet areas; semi-infaunal.
Localities: Entire.
Occurrence: Common.
Range: Cape Cod to Florida; Gulf states; Costa Rica; West Indies; Brazil.
Remarks: These scavenging "mud snails" common on flats but most move to deeper water in winter; eggs laid in gelatinous capsules attached to bottom.

Size: 51–100 mm.
Color: Background cream with irregular purplish brown and orange brown mottlings; widely spaced, rarely broken, brown spiral bands.
Shape: Elongate fusiform.
Ornament or sculpture: 7 to 9 rounded whorls; smooth near well-defined sutures; spiral striations on base and fine transverse growth lines.
Aperture: Long oval, glazed white inside; outer lip thin, brownish with numerous raised white threads on inner surface; parietal area thinly glazed with white; moderately long siphonal canal open; incurved columella has strong plication toward end.
Habitat: Inlet areas and offshore; epifaunal.
Localities: Entire, more to south.
Occurrence: Fairly common.
Range: North Carolina to western Gulf of Mexico.

Remarks: Uses its strong foot to jump out of unwary collector's pocket; eggs in vase-shaped capsules attached to shell, pilings, and other structures; referred to as *F. hunteria* Perry, 1811.

True Tulip Shell
Fasciolaria (Fasciolaria) tulipa (Linné, 1758) [See *SST*, p. 145]

Genus *Pleuroploca* P. Fischer, 1884

Florida Horse Conch
Pleuroploca gigantea (Kiener, 1840)

Size: Up to 150–225 mm.
Color: Dirty white to chalky salmon; juveniles bright orange.
Shape: Fusiform.
Ornament or sculpture: About 8 convex whorls; sutures distinct; spiral sculpture of strong, irregularly spaced cords, with finer threads between; transverse growth lines.
Aperture: Oval, polished, orange colored; outer lip thin, slightly crenulate; columella has 2 plicae near base; siphonal canal long, upturned.

Habitat: Offshore and in inlet areas; epifaunal.
Localities: Entire.
Occurrence: Uncommon.
Range: North Carolina to both sides of Florida; Texas; Campeche Bank.
Remarks: Largest shell found on Texas coast; old specimens usually covered with calcareous bryozoa; faded and worn even when living; found living on jetty at Port Aransas.

Family MELONGENIDAE Gill, 1871 = [GALEODIDAE Thiele, 1925]
Subfamily BUSYCONINAE Finlay & Marwick, 1937

Genus *Busycon* Röding, 1798

Pear Whelk
Busycon spiratum plagosum (Conrad, 1863)

Size: 75–100 mm.
Color: Creamy with irregular brown axial lines.
Shape: Pyriform.
Ornament or sculpture: Spire whorls turreted, producing step at each suture; suture boxlike; sharp carina at shoulder finely beaded; spiral sculpture of fine threads.

Aperture: Pyriform; outer lip thin; interior strongly striate, rosy brown except near lip, where it is white; siphonal canal long, nearly straight.
Habitat: Offshore and inlet areas in sandy bottoms to 7.2 meters (4 fathoms); infaunal.
Localities: Entire.
Occurrence: Fairly common.
Range: Mobile Bay to Campeche Bay.
Remarks: At times these whelks found living on sand bars in inlet areas where they will "pop up" after extended low tides; egg capsules smaller than those of *B. p. pulleyi* and have crenulated edges; bivalves main food source.

Subgenus *Sinistrofulgur* Hollister, 1950

Lightning Whelk
Busycon (Sinistrofulgur) perversum pulleyi Hollister, 1958

Size: 100–200 mm.
Color: Pale fawn to light yellowish gray with long axial, wavy brown streaks; large adults usually lose color.
Shape: Pyriform, sinistral.
Ornament or sculpture: Body whorl large, spire one-fifth height of shell; spire turreted, sutures slightly below shoulder; fine spiral threads; colored growth lines correspond with spines that circle shoulder.

Aperture: Pyriform; outer lip thin, edged in purplish brown; interior pale yellow to light orange; siphonal canal long, somewhat twisted and recurved.
Habitat: Intertidal, offshore, in bays; infaunal.
Localities: Entire.
Occurrence: Common.
Range: Brenton Sound, Louisiana, to Texas and northern Mexican coast.
Remarks: This carnivore can be caught in bays with crab lines when it comes to feed on bait; buries itself in sand with siphonal canal protruding; feeds on mollusks, opening bivalves by chipping valve edges with own shell until it can insert proboscis; constructs long strings of horny, disc-shaped capsules up to size of quarter with black-colored foot, attaching them to substratum; much confusion exists as to name of Texas species of *Busycon*.

Family COLUMBELLIDAE Swainson, 1840 = [PYRENIDAE Suter, 1913]

Genus *Anachis* H. & A. Adams, 1853
Subgenus *Costoanachis* Sacco, 1890

Semiplicate Dove Shell
Anachis (Costoanachis) semiplicata Stearns, 1873

Size: 8–15 mm.
Color: Yellow gray or whitish with reddish brown, irregular markings.

Shape: Fusiform.
Ornament or sculpture: Spire slightly more than one-half of shell length; whorls almost flat-sided; sutures shallow; body whorl narrow; sculpture of small number of widely spaced, low axial ribs limited to body whorl; spire smooth.
Aperture: Moderately wide; outer lip barely thickened, distinctly denticulate interiorly; columella straight with obsolete denticulations.
Habitat: On broken shell and rocks in sandy areas; epifaunal.
Localities: Entire.
Occurrence: Common.
Range: Southwestern Florida; Gulf of Mexico to Progreso, Yucatán.
Remarks: Several species reported as being found in Texas; *A. floridana* Rehder, 1939, and *A. lafresnayi* (Fischer & Bernardi, 1856), formerly *A. translirata* (Ravenel, 1861), often mentioned.

Subgenus *Parvanachis* Radwin, 1968

Fat Dove Shell
Anachis (Parvanachis) ostreiocola
Sowerby, 1882

Size: 4–5 mm.
Color: Variable: some whitish with dark brown bands, others solid reddish brown.

Shape: Ovate conic; short fusiform.
Ornament or sculpture: 5 convex whorls, stout, rotund; spiral sculpture of strong spiral cords that do not cross transverse ribs, giving reticulated pattern.
Aperture: Oval, oblique; outer lip thickened in adults with denticulations on inner edge; base of columella denticulate.
Habitat: Under shell on sandy bottoms and oyster reefs; epifaunal.
Localities: Entire.
Occurrence: Common.
Range: Bermuda; Virginia to Florida; Gulf states; Costa Rica; West Indies; Surinam; Brazil.
Remarks: *A. ostreicola* is probably a variety of *A. obesa*; they differ in the proportion of body whorl to spire. *A. ostreicola* has less flaring apertural lip, greater overall convexity of spire, uniform and distinct overall color pattern, and stronger spiral sculpture; lives on oyster reefs in shallow mud-bottom areas, whereas *A. obesa* prefers deeper water on sand bottoms; *A. ostreicola* ranges Gulf of Mexico for Key West, Florida, to South Texas.

Genus *Mitrella* Risso, 1826
Subgenus *Astyris* H. & A. Adams, 1853

Lunar Dove Shell
Mitrella (Astyris) lunata (Say, 1826)

Size: 5 mm.
Color: Glossy white to cream with numerous fine, zigzag brown markings; occasional specimens have brown markings in definite spiral bands.
Shape: Ovate conic.
Ornament or sculpture: Smooth with about 5 flat-sided, tapering whorls; spiral striations on base of shell.
Aperture: Long oval; outer lip thin on edge, denticulated on interior; columella short; edge of siphonal canal dark brown.
Habitat: High-salinity shell reef just below low-tide mark, grass flats, inlets; epifaunal.
Localities: Entire.
Occurrence: Fairly common.
Range: Bermuda; Massachusetts to Florida; Texas; Carmen, Campeche, Mexico; Gulf of Campeche; Yucatán; West Indies; Surinam; northern and northeastern Brazil.
Remarks: Some marked below sutures in spiral bands of white followed by brown dots and oblique lines; may belong in genus *Anachis*, subgenus *Alia*.

Family MURICIDAE Rafinesque, 1815
Subfamily MURICINAE da Costa, 1776
Genus *Murex* Linné, 1758
Subgenus *Hexaplex* Perry, 1810

Giant Eastern Murex
Murex (Hexaplex) fulvescens
G. B. Sowerby I, 1834

Size: 125–150 mm.
Color: Milky white to dirty gray with reddish brown blotches with spiral threads.
Shape: Conic; extended siphonal canal.
Ornament or sculpture: 6 to 7 convex, heavy whorls; suture distinct, irregular; spire short; spiral sculpture of strong, brown cords that connect corresponding spines to each varix, numerous raised threads between them; transverse sculpture of 6 to 10 highly spinous varices.
Aperture: Oval to subcircular; outer lip crenulated, thickened into very spinose varix; parietal lip glazed with low ridge at upper part; siphonal canal fairly short, broad; previous canals form series of flutings terminating in false umbilicus; interior porcelaneous white.
Habitat: On jetties and just offshore or in inlet areas; semi-infaunal.
Localities: Entire.
Occurrence: Fairly common.
Range: North Carolina; Florida to Texas; northern Mexico.
Remarks: Deposits eggs in rubbery capsules attached to some substratum; larvae have nonpelagic development.

Subgenus *Phyllonotus* Swainson, 1833

Apple Murex
Murex (Phyllonotus) pomum (Gmelin, 1791)

Size: 51–112 mm.
Color: Dark brown to yellowish tan with irregular dark brown spiral bands, which are often reduced to spots.
Shape: Conic with slightly extended siphonal canal.
Ornament or sculpture: 7 to 9 solid, convex whorls; suture not always distinct; spire extended; spiral sculpture of series of strong cords; scaly cords form nodules on ridges, several finer scaly threads between them; transverse sculpture of 3 prominent, equidistant varices on each whorl; each varix has row of low, open spines and fluted edge on forward margin; several ridges between varices.
Aperture: Oval to subcircular, large; interior polished, colored pink or ivory, yellow, orange; outer lip thin, crenulate with varix bordering outer edge; spotted brown to correspond with spiral bands; parietal area glazed, adheres to body whorls, except for erect edge; siphon short, slightly recurved; dark brown spot on upper end of parietal wall.
Habitat: Gravelly bottom, 5.4 to 12.6 meters (3 to 7 fathoms); semi-infaunal.
Localities: Entire.
Occurrence: Uncommon beach shell.
Range: North Carolina to Florida; Texas; Campeche Bank; Yucatán; West Indies; Surinam; Brazil.
Remarks: This carnivore bores into shell of prey; eggs deposited in yellowish, leathery, tongue-shaped, massed capsules; old shells occupied by hermit crabs occasionally found in inlet areas.

Subfamily THAIDINAE Suter, 1913

Genus *Thais* Röding, 1798
Subgenus *Stramonita* Schumaker, 1817

Hays' Rock Shell
Thais (Stramonita) haemastoma canaliculata (Gray, 1839)

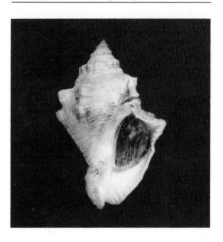

Size: Up to 112 mm.
Color: Grayish with irregular mottling of darker color in either axial or spiral pattern.
Shape: Conic.
Ornament or sculpture: 7 to 8 convex, solid whorls; sutures usually indented; body whorl has angled shoulder; spiral sculpture of numerous, coarse, incised lines with 2 rows of large nodules on whorl shoulder; transverse sculpture of fine growth lines.
Aperture: Subovate; outer lip thickened with crenulations that run into aperture; interior light brownish to pinkish orange; parietal lip glazed, thickened by inductura; ridge at upper edge runs into aperture; may be weak plicae on base of straight columella; siphonal canal short, oblique; umbilicus closed.
Habitat: Shallow water on rocks or oyster reefs; epifaunal.
Localities: Entire.
Occurrence: Fairly common.

Range: Bermuda; Gulf of Mexico from Florida west to Texas.
Remarks: *T. h. canaliculata* and *T. h. haysae* may only be variations of *T. h. floridana*; in other areas this mollusk serious oyster pest.

Florida Rock Shell
Thais (Stramonita) haemastoma floridana (Conrad, 1837)

Size: 51–75 mm.
Color: Light gray to yellowish, mottled with darker color in axial pattern.
Shape: Conic.
Ornament or sculpture: 6 to 7 convex whorls. Sutures in rather heavy shell fine, occasionally indented; sculpture quite variable; spiral sculpture may consist of incised lines and 2 rows of small nodules; transverse sculpture of fine growth lines; shoulders may be angled or not.
Aperture: Subovate; interior salmon pink; outer lip dark brown between denticulations that run into interior of aperture; parietal lip glazed, smooth, thickened by inductura; columella straight, may have faint plicae near base; anal canal short with ridge along parietal wall; siphonal canal short, oblique; umbilicus closed.
Habitat: Intertidal on rocks; epifaunal.

Localities: Entire.
Occurrence: Common.
Range: North Carolina to Florida; Texas; Yucatán; Central America; West Indies; northern and northeastern Brazil.
Remarks: Carnivorous on bivalves; lays eggs in purplish capsules clustered together on rocks, cans, bottles, etc.

Family OLIVIDAE Latreille, 1825
Subfamily OLIVINAE Swainson, 1840

Genus *Oliva* Bruguière, 1789
Subgenus *Ispidula* Gray, 1847

Lettered Olive
Oliva (Ispidula) sayana Ravenel, 1834

Size: 51–62 mm.
Color: Polished cream-colored background with numerous brownish zigzag markings.
Shape: Elongate oval.
Ornament or sculpture: 5 to 6 whorls; body whorl dominates shell; spire short, acute; sutures deep.
Aperture: Long, narrow, purplish within; outer lip thin; siphonal canal oblique notch at base; white columella plicated.
Habitat: Inlets and offshore; infaunal.
Localities: Entire.
Occurrence: Common.

Range: North Carolina to Florida; Gulf states; West Indies; Brazil.
Remarks: Skin divers find this nocturnal predator plowing along just under sand; shell covered with propodium and lateral folds of foot; in warm months feeds on *Donax*, occasionally on *Polinices duplicatus*, in winter reduces feeding and depends on scavenging.

Genus *Olivella* Swainson, 1831

Whitened Dwarf Olive
Olivella dealbata (Reeve, 1850)

Size: 6–9 mm.
Color: Glossy white or cream; body whorl faintly marked with brownish zigzag streaks; color variable.
Shape: Elongate oval.
Ornament or sculpture: Smooth; sutures distinct, slightly canaliculated; fasciole at base of shell white, bounded with fine raised thread.
Aperture: Long, narrow, about three-fourths length of body whorl; outer lip thin; parietal inductura well developed; columella slightly concave with 7 to 9 weak oblique plications; siphonal notch not as pronounced as in *O. minuta*.
Habitat: Inlet areas in sand; infaunal.
Localities: Entire, more to east.
Occurrence: Common.
Range: North Carolina to both sides of Florida; Texas; Yucatán; West Indies.

Remarks: At times in winter months can be found by thousands in drift on outer beaches; closely related to *O. floralia* Duclos, 1835, and may be only a form of it.

Subgenus *Niteoliva* Olsson, 1956

Minute Dwarf Olive
Olivella (Niteoliva) minuta (Link, 1807)

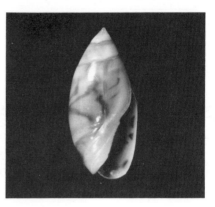

Size: 6–12 mm.
Color: Polished grayish white background with purplish brown zigzag line on body whorl and fine brown lines along sutures; color variable.
Shape: Elongate oval.
Ornament or sculpture: Very smooth; apex acute; sutures open and grooved but not as pronounced as in *O. dealbata*; fine spiral line above base.
Aperture: Long, narrow, about three-fourths length of body whorl; outer lip thin; columella slightly concave with weak oblique plications; pronounced siphonal notch.
Habitat: Inlets and surf zone; infaunal.
Localities: Entire, more to south.
Occurrence: Common at times.
Range: Texas; Costa Rica; Caribbean; West Indies; Brazil.
Remarks: At low tide during full moon, carry a lantern to find this nocturnal carnivore plowing along under sand in inlet areas; may be *O. mutica* Dall & Simpson, 1901.

Family MARGINELLIDAE Fleming, 1828

Genus *Prunum* Herrmannsen, 1852
Subgenus *Leptegouana* Woodring, 1928

Common Atlantic Marginella
Prunum (Leptegouana) apicina Menke, 1828

Size: 12 mm.
Color: Polished cream, yellowish, or grayish tan with several reddish brown spots on outer lip.
Shape: Conic, broad anteriorly.
Ornament or sculpture: Smooth; spire short; convex body whorl large.
Aperture: Long, narrow, length of body whorl; outer lip thickened, notched at base; columella with 4 strong plicae below.
Habitat: Shallow, grassy, inlet-influenced areas; epifaunal.
Localities: Port Aransas, south.
Occurrence: Uncommon in beach drift.
Range: North Carolina to Florida; Gulf states; Yucatán; West Indies.
Remarks: Probably fossil; [*Marginella apicina*].

Subclass EUTHYNEURA Spengel, 1881
= [OPISTHOBRANCHIA Milne Edwards, 1848, and PULMONATA Cuvier, 1817]
Order SACOGLOSSA Von Ihering, 1876 = [ASCOGLOSSA Bergh, 1877]
Superfamily ELYSIACEA H. & A. Adams, 1854
Family ELYSIIDAE H. & A. Adams, 1854

Genus *Elysia* Risso, 1818

Elysia sp. [See *SST*, p. 156]

Order DORIDOIDEA Odhner, 1934 = [HOLOHEPATICA Bergh, 1881]
Suborder CRYPTOBRANCHIA Fischer, 1883 = [EUDORIDOIDEA Odhner, 1934]
Superfamily DORIDACEA Rafinesque, 1815
Family DORIDIDAE Rafinesque, 1815
Subfamily DISCODORIDINAE Bergh, 1891

Genus *Discodoris* Bergh, 1877

Discodoris hedgpethi Marcus & Marcus, 1959 [See *SST*, p. 156]

Suborder PHANEROBRANCHIA Von Ihering, 1876
Superfamily ONCHIDORIDACEA Alder & Hancock, 1845 = [SUCTORIA Bergh, 1892]
Family CORAMBIDAE Bergh, 1869

Genus *Doridella* Verrill, 1870

Doridella obscura Verrill, 1870 [See *SST*, p. 157]

Order DENDRONOTOIDEA Odhner,
1936
Family SCYLLAEIDAE Rafinesque,
1815

Genus *Scyllaea* Linné, 1758

Sargassum Nudibranch
Scyllaea pelagica Linné, 1758

Order EOLIDOIDEA Odhner, 1937
Suborder EOLIDOIDEA Odhner, 1968
Infraorder ACLEIOPROCTA Odhner,
1939
Family FIONIDAE Gray, 1837

Genus *Fiona* Forbes & Hanley, 1851

Atlantic Blue Fiona
Fiona pinnata (Eschscholtz, 1831)

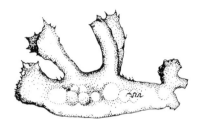

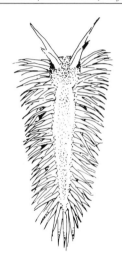

Size: 25–51 mm.
Color: Yellowish brown to orange
brown, *Sargassum* colored.
Shape: Sluglike.
Ornament or sculpture: No oral
tentacles; 2 slender, long rhinophores;
2 series of large foliaceous gill plumes,
or cerata, on each side of body.
Aperture: None.
Habitat: Pelagic in *Sargassum*;
epifaunal.
Localities: Entire.
Occurrence: Common.
Range: Southeastern United States;
other warm seas.
Remarks: Found clinging to *Sargassum*,
along with at least 4 other unidentified
nudibranchs; will live in aquarium for
days, a delight to watch; eggs laid in
zigzag, yellow gelatinous strings.

Size: 39 mm.
Color: Variable: reddish, bluish,
yellowish.
Shape: Sluglike.
Ornament or sculpture: Margins of
foot broad, extending beyond body
sides; cerata densely situated along
margins of notum, leaving large part of
back clear; each of larger cerata has
conspicuous longitudinal membrane
along posterolateral axis, containing
undulating blood vessel.
Aperture: None.
Habitat: Pelagic on floating seaweed.
Localities: Entire.
Occurrence: Seasonally common.
Range: Gulf Stream; Alaska to Peru.
Remarks: Brought in by spring winds;
feeds on *Velella* coelenterates and
Lepas barnacles; syn. *F. nobilis* (Alder
& Hancock, 1848).

Infraorder CLEIOPROCTA Odhner, 1939
Family FAVORINIDAE Bergh, 1889
Subfamily FAVORININAE Bergh, 1889

Genus *Cratena* Bergh, 1864

Cratena pilata Gould, 1870 [See *SST*, p. 158]

Family EOLIDIIDAE Orbigny, 1834

Genus *Spurilla* Bergh, 1864

Spurilla neapolitana (Delle Chiaje, 1823)

(after E. du B.-R. Marcus and E. Marcus, *Pub. Inst. Marine Sci.* 6:251–254 [1959])

Size: 20–40 mm.
Color: Colorful, varying from ivory, yellowish rose, or pinkish with reddish brown to olive green diverticula within cerata, which are tipped with white and keeled on side facing midline; opaque white dots on cerata, head, back.
Shape: Elongate, tapered posteriorly; sluglike.
Ornament or sculpture: Rows of arched cerata on dorsal surface.
Aperture: None.
Habitat: On weeds attached to floating logs; pelagic.
Localities: Probably entire.

Occurrence: Occasionally common.
Range: Florida to Texas; Caribbean to Brazil; eastern Atlantic; Mediterranean.
Remarks: First collected in Texas by Joel W. Hedgpeth at Port Aransas on June 25, 1948; feeds on sea anemones.

Genus *Berghia* Trinchese, 1877

Berghia coerulescens (Laurillard, 1831) [See *SST*, p. 159]

Genus *Cerberilla* Bergh, 1873

Cerberilla tanna Marcus & Marcus, 1959 [See *SST*, p. 160]

Family GLAUCIDAE Menke, 1828

Genus *Glaucus* Forster, 1777

Blue Glaucus
Glaucus atlanticus Forster, 1777

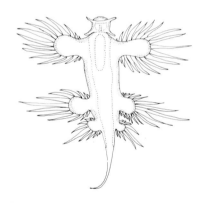

Size: 51 mm.
Color: Shades of blue.
Shape: Sluglike body.
Ornament or sculpture: Tentacles and rhinophores small; 4 clumps of bright blue frilled cerata on each side of body.
Aperture: None.
Habitat: Pelagic in warm seas.
Localities: Entire.
Occurrence: Occasionally common.

Range: Worldwide.
Remarks: This brightly colored slug washed ashore by strong southeast winds in spring when *Janthina* coming in; feeds on siphonophores.

Order PLEUROBRANCHIA
  Von Ihering, 1922
Superfamily PLEUROBRANCHACEA
  Menke, 1828
Family PLEUROBRANCHIDAE
  Menke, 1828
Subfamily PLEUROBRANCHINAE
  Menke, 1828

Genus *Pleurobranchaea* Leve, 1813

Pleurobranchaea hedgpethi Abbott,
  1952 [See *SST*, p. 161]

Order STEGANOBRANCHIA Von
  Ihering, 1876
Suborder ACTEONOIDEA Orbigny,
  1835
Superfamily ACTEONACEA Orbigny,
  1835
Family ACTEONIDAE Orbigny, 1835

Genus *Acteon* Monfort, 1810

Adam's Baby-Bubble
Acteon punctostriatus (C.B. Adams,
  1840)

Size: 3–6 mm.
Color: White, fragile.
Shape: Globose, conic.
Ornament or sculpture: 4 convex whorls; sutures deep; spire elevated; body whorl large with fine spiral striations over basal half.
Aperture: Elongated pear shape; outer lip thin; little more than one-half length of body whorl; columella short with one strong oblique fold.
Habitat: Inlet areas and outer beaches; infaunal.
Localities: Entire.
Occurrence: Fairly common.
Range: Gulf of Mexico; Gulf of Campeche; Campeche Bank; Brazil.
Remarks: This vermivore burrows just below surface of sand. [*Rictaxis punctostriatus*]

Suborder BULLOIDEA Lamarck, 1801
Superfamily BULLACEA Lamarck,
  1801
Family BULLIDAE Lamarck, 1801

Genus *Bulla* Linné, 1758

Striate Bubble
Bulla striata Bruguière, 1792

Size: 18–25 mm.
Color: Whitish with small irregular mottlings of chocolate brown.
Shape: Oval with sunken spire.
Ornament or sculpture: Delicate shell smooth except for microscopic growth

lines; spiral sculpture of fine grooves toward base and within sunken apical end.
Aperture: Longer than body whorl, wider near base; interior whitish; outer lip thin; parietal area covered with glazed white inductura.
Habitat: Inlet areas on grass in shallow water; epifaunal.
Localities: Entire.
Occurrence: Common.
Range: Bermuda; western coast of Florida to Texas; Yucatán; Costa Rica; West Indies to Brazil.
Remarks: Mantle of this carnivore completely envelops shell; photosensitive; burrows in grass roots; eggs in gelatinous ribbons.

Family ACTEOCINIDAE Pilsbry, 1921

Genus *Acteocina* Gray, 1847

Channeled Barrel-Bubble
Acteocina candei (d'Orbigny, 1841)

Size: 3.6 mm.
Color: Glossy white.
Shape: Cylindrical with moderately elevated spire.
Ornament or sculpture: Smooth except for axial ribbing on sub-sutural band.
Aperture: Long, narrow, wider at base; outer lip thin; columella single, raised fold below parietal inductura.
Habitat: Near-shore oceanic conditions.

Localities: Entire.
Occurrence: Common in beach drift.
Range: Cape Hatteras to Florida; Texas; Campeche Bank; West Indies; Surinam.
Remarks: Gelatinous egg masses attached to marine grasses; nonpelagic veligers; [*Retusa canaliculata*].
More cylindrical and much smaller than the common *A. canaliculata* Say, 1826, an extremely similar and often confused estuarine species.

Orbigny's Baby-Bubble
Acteocina bidentata (Orbigny, 1841)

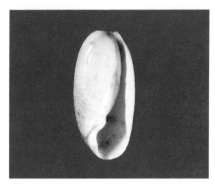

Size: 2.5–4 mm.
Color: White, fragile.
Shape: Cylindrical.
Ornament or sculpture: Smooth; spire depressed; body whorl narrowed above and below.
Aperture: Long, narrow; outer lip thin, slightly flared below; columella short with 2 plicae at base.
Habitat: Inlet areas near low-water mark; infaunal.
Localities: Entire.
Occurrence: Fairly common.
Range: North Carolina; Florida; Gulf states; Yucatán; West Indies; Brazil.
Remarks: Maculated mantle of this minute carnivore envelops shell; crawls just under sand leaving a raised trail. Syn. *Cylinchnella bidentata*.

Family ATYIDAE Thiele, 1926

Genus *Haminoea* Turton & Kingston, 1830

Elegant Paper-Bubble
Haminoea antillarum (Orbigny, 1841)

Size: 18 mm.
Color: Pale greenish yellow, almost translucent.
Shape: Rounded oval; spire insunk.
Ornament or sculpture: Surface appears smooth but has fine growth striae and microscopic, wavy, spiral lines.
Aperture: Longer than body whorl, wider at bottom; outer lip arises to right of apical depression; columella extremely concave; parietal area has narrow white inductura.
Habitat: Inlet-influenced areas in shallow water; epifaunal.
Localities: Entire.
Occurrence: Fairly common.
Range: Gulf of Mexico; Yucatán; West Indies; northeastern Brazil.
Remarks: This carnivore cannot withdraw into shell; varies diet with algae.

Conrad's Paper-Bubble
Haminoea succinea (Conrad, 1846)

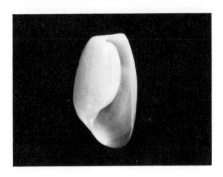

Size: 10 mm.
Color: White to pale amber.
Shape: Cylindrical, thin; spire insunk.
Ornament or sculpture: Surface covered with minute, wavy, spiral lines.
Aperture: Longer than body whorl, wider near base; outer lip thin, sharp; columella concave with one weak fold above center.
Habitat: Inlet influence in shallow water; epifaunal.
Localities: Entire.
Occurrence: Uncommon to rare in beach drift.
Range: Bermuda; Florida to Texas; Campeche Bank.
Remarks: Animal brown.

Genus *Volvulella* Newton, 1891

Volvulella persimilis (Mörch, 1875) [See *SST*, p. 164]

Subgenus *Paravolvulella* Harry, 1967

Volvulella (Paravolvulella) texasiana Harry, 1967 [See *SST*, p. 164]

Suborder APLYSIOIDEA Lamarck, 1809
Infraorder LONGICOMMISSURATA Pruvot-Fol, 1954
Superfamily APLYSIACEA Lamarck, 1809
Family APLYSIIDAE Rafinesque, 1815
Subfamily APLYSIINAE Rafinesque, 1815

Genus *Aplysia* Linné, 1767
Subgenus *Varria* Eales, 1960

Mottled Sea Hare
Aplysia (Varria) brasiliana Rang, 1828

(swimming)

(G. W. Tryon, Jr., *Manual of Conchology* [Philadelphia: Acad. Natur. Sci., 1895] 16:pl. 35)

Size: 100–225 mm.
Exudate: Reddish purple.
Shell: Narrow to broad, concave, dark yellow, with apex hard and hooked but without spire; internal.
Body: Very variable; large, bulky, self-colored or spotted; tough skin; simple cephalic tentacles; slender rhinophores set close together; long neck; narrow foot; long tapering verge; very large parapodia joined low down posteriorly; mantle aperture tubular; opaline gland compound, uniporous; simple radula.
Habitat: Bays and offshore reefs where algae grows; epifaunal.
Localities: Entire.
Occurrence: Common.
Range: New Jersey to Brazil; St. Helena; Ghana.
Remarks: Syn. *A. floridensis* (Pilsbry, 1895) and *A. willcoxi* Helprin, 1886; more abundant in warm months; this unusual creature observed swimming between jetties at Port Aransas and South Padre with head breaking surface of water; does well in aquariums; eggs deposited in tangled mass of gelatinous ribbons on grass flats, usually dark green to light brown; currently subject of expanded field and laboratory culture studies because of importance in neurophysiological and behavioral studies.

(inner shell)

Spotted Sea Hare
Aplysia (Varria) dactylomela Rang,
 1828

Sooty Sea Hare
Aplysia (Varria) morio Verrill, 1901

(after P. C. S. A. L. Rang, "Histoire
naturelle des Aplysiens . . . ," in
*Histoire naturelle gen. et partic. des
mollusques-pteropodes*, ed. Ferussac
[1828], pl. 9)

Size: 100–125 mm.
Exudate: Deep purple.
Shell: Large, broad, rounded, with
oblique apex; strongly calcified, with
hardly any trace of spire; internal.
Body: Bulky; basic yellowish green
color, with numerous large black rings
of irregular sizes on sides; thick
rhinophores with short notched apices;
broad foot with blunt tail; frilled
swimming lobes joined low down
posteriorly; broad spatulate spirally
grooved verge; compound uniporous
opaline gland; lateral teeth of radula
with long straight smooth cusps.
Habitat: Where algae grow
abundantly; epifaunal.
Localities: Port Isabel.
Occurrence: Uncommon, late fall and
winter.
Range: Circumtropical.
Remarks: Syn. *A. protea* Rang, 1828;
lifespan 1 year.

Size: 212–318 mm.
Exudate: Purple.
Shell: Long and narrow without spire,
strongly ridged, hardly any anal sinus;
internal.
Body: Bulky; dark purple to black;
wide hemispherical tentacles; narrow
foot with short tail; very large, free,
thin, swimming parapodia, arising close
behind rhinophores, becoming wide,
rounded and fluted on edges, uniting
low down on tail; mantle and visceral
regions small; no shell foramen in
adult; large leaflike siphon, large
cteniduium, simple multiporous opaline
gland; radula with numerous rows and
more than 50 teeth on each side;
elaborate denticulation; verge sheath
anchored by numerous muscle strands,
plain internally; verge short, stout,
unpigmented.
Habitat: Where algae grow
abundantly; epifaunal.
Localities: South Padre.
Occurrence: Common sporadically
during summer.
Range: Rhode Island to Texas; Bermuda
and the West Indies.
Remarks: Excellent swimmer.

Aplysia (Varria) donca Marcus &
 Marcus, 1959 [See *SST*, p. 166]

Infraorder BREVICOMMISSURATA
Pruvot-Fol, 1954
Subfamily DOLABRIFERINAE Pilsbry,
1895

Genus *Bursatella* Blainville, 1817

Ragged Sea Hare
Bursatella leachii pleii (Rang, 1828)

(Tryon 1895, 16:pl. 43)

Size: 100 mm.
Exudate: Not defined.
Body: Olive green to gray, usually with white specks; covered with numerous ragged appendages.
Shell: None in adult.
Habitat: Where algae grow abundantly.
Localities: South Padre.
Occurrence: Uncommon, late fall and winter.
Range: Worldwide circumtropical.
Remarks: First reported in Texas by Breuer (1962); form common to Gulf of Mexico just one of a number of subspecies.

Order ENTOMOTAENIATA
Cossmann, 1896
Superfamily PYRAMIDELLACEA
Gray, 1840
Family PYRAMIDELLIDAE Gray, 1840

Genus *Pyramidella* Lamarck, 1799
Subgenus *Longchaeus* Mörch, 1875

Notched Pyram
Pyramidella (Longchaeus) crenulata
(Holmes, 1859)

Size: 10–12 mm.
Color: Pale brown; cream to white when dead; polished.
Shape: Elongate conic.
Ornament or sculpture: Numerous flat-sided whorls; sutures distinct, V-shaped channels; spire acute; body whorl rounded at base; posterior margin of each whorl delicately crenulated; weak basal line meets outer lip at suture; phaneromphalous.
Aperture: Small, rather auriform, entire; outer lip thin; columella sinuous, 2 oblique folds.
Habitat: Ectoparasitic in inlets and hypersaline lagoons; epifaunal.
Localities: Entire.
Occurrence: Common.
Range: South Carolina to Florida; Texas; West Indies.
Remarks: Largest pyram on this coast.

69

Genus *Boonea* Robertson, 1978

Impressed Odostome
Boonea impressa (Say, 1822)

Size: 4–6 mm.
Color: Whitish.
Shape: Elongate conic.
Ornament or sculpture: 8 flattened whorls, shouldered above; sutures channeled; nuclear whorls small, partly imbedded in first succeeding turn; spiral sculpture of 3 strong deeply cut grooves; grooves cut by spiral threads; base rounded, spirally grooved.
Aperture: Ovate; outer lip thin, slightly sinuous at edge, showing external sculpture within; columella stout with strong oblique plica at insertion.
Habitat: Ectoparasitic on oyster reefs; epifaunal.
Localities: Entire.
Occurrence: Common.
Range: New Jersey to Quintana Roo.
Remarks: Most common *Boonea* on Texas coast; because it feeds on *Crassostrea virginica*, this ectoparasite has been studied considerably; also feeds on *Diastoma*, *Crepidula*, and oyster drills; according to Robert Robertson, the Texas species may be different from the one in North Carolina, although they seem to have identical shells; a North Carolina population has pelagic larvae, while a Texas population has nonpelagic larvae; probably syn. *Odostomia trifida* Totten, 1834; [*Odostomia impressa*].

Half-Smooth Odostome
Boonea seminuda (C. B. Adams, 1839)

Size: 4 mm.
Color: Whitish.
Shape: Elongate conic.
Ornament or sculpture: 6 to 7 slightly convex whorls; whorls shouldered; sutures distinct; whorls sculptured between sutures by axial ribs cancellated into beads or nodules by 4 low, broad, equidistant ridges; base of body whorl spirally grooved.
Aperture: Auriform; outer lip thick inside but edge thin, entire; columella strong, twisted, reflexed with oblique plica.
Habitat: Ectoparasitic in bays and on shallow shelf; epifaunal.
Localities: Entire.
Occurrence: Fairly common.
Range: Prince Edward Island, Canada, to Texas.
Remarks: Nonspecific ectoparasite known to feed on *Crepidula* and *Pecten*; can stand less saline waters than some of the other *Boonea*; holes in dead specimens indicate that gastropods feed on it in turn.

Genus *Fargoa* Bartsch, 1955
Fargoa cf. *F. bushiana* (Bartsch, 1909)

Fat Odostome
Fargoa gibbosa (Bush, 1909)

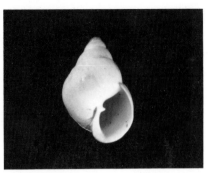

Size: 1.8–3 mm.
Color: White.
Shape: Elongate conic.
Ornament or sculpture: 4 postnuclear whorls; each whorl bears 3 rows of tubercles and smooth spiral keel just above suture.
Aperture: Obliquely oval or pear-shaped; 1 plica on columella.
Habitat: Ectoparasitic in bays; epifaunal.
Localities: Entire.
Occurrence: Fairly common in beach drift.
Range: Massachusetts to São Paulo, Brazil.
Remarks: Called *Odostomia dux* in *SST*, p. 171, but *O. dux* is not a synonym; it is a name that has been misapplied to the species.

Size: 3 mm.
Color: Whitish, polished.
Shape: Globose conic.
Ornament or sculpture: About 5 very convex whorls; shell rather fragile; sutures distinct; smooth except for microscopic growth striations.
Aperture: Pear-shaped, fairly large; outer lip thin; columella marked with single prominent tooth near insertion.
Habitat: Ectoparasitic in inlet areas; epifaunal.
Localities: Entire.
Occurrence: Fairly common in beach drift.
Range: Connecticut; North Carolina; Louisiana; Texas.
Remarks: Rounded shape of shell distinguishes it from other *Fargoa*.

Fargoa dianthophila (Wells & Wells, 1961)

Size: 1.8 mm.
Remarks: Found in Texas but not described or figured in *SST*. [Figured in *Biol. Bull.* 155:366, Oct. 1978.]

Genus *Odostomia* Fleming, 1817
Subgenus *Evalea* A. Adams, 1860

? *Odostomia (Evalea)* cf. *O. emeryi*
(Bartsch, 1955)

Genus *Sayella* Dall, 1885

? *Sayella* cf. *S. livida* Rehder, 1935

Size: 2.9 mm.
Color: Cream yellow.
Shape: Elongate conic.
Ornament or sculpture: Thin; nuclear
whorls small, obliquely immersed in
first postnuclear turn; postnuclear
whorls well rounded and crossed by
numerous microscopic spiral lines;
suture deeply impressed; base inflated,
rounded, strongly umbilicated.
Aperture: Large, oval; columella
slender, curved with internal spiral cord
near insertion; parietal wall covered
with thin inductura; outer lip thin,
strongly curved; rounded body whorl
distinctive.
Habitat: Uncertain.
Localities: San Luis Pass and south.
Occurrence: Uncommon in beach drift.
Range: Undetermined; known from
Pliocene of North St. Petersburg,
Florida.
Remarks: Fold on columella places
species among *Pyramidellas*, but has
not been definitely identified.

Size: 3.5−4 mm.
Color: Straw yellow with wide
subsutural white band.
Shape: Elongate conic.
Ornament or sculpture: About 6½
moderately convex whorls; smooth
except for microscopic growth lines
and spiral sculpture; whorls closely
adpressed at suture; body whorl half of
shell length, suture considerably below
periphery of preceding whorl.
Aperture: Small, obliquely ovate; lip
thin, thickened anteriorly, proceeding
into base of columella, which bears a
strong fold; area surrounding base of
columella reddish brown.
Habitat: Ectoparasitic in bays and inlet
areas; epifaunal.
Localities: Central, probably entire.
Occurrence: Fairly common in beach
drift.
Range: Florida; Texas.
Remarks: Identification only a guess; if
correct, holotype collected by J. A.
Singley in Corpus Christi Bay, Texas, in
1893.

Mesh-Pitted Chiton

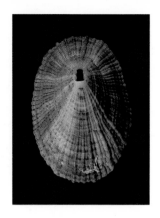

Keyhole Limpet

Sculptured Top-Shell

Checkered Pheasant

Antillean Nerite

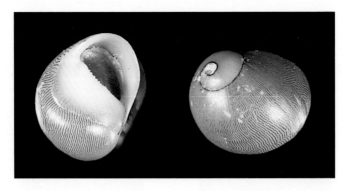

Olive Nerite

Virgin Nerite

Emerald Nerite

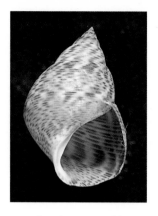

Angulate Periwinkle

Marsh Periwinkle

Zebra Periwinkle

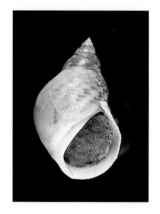

Cloudy Periwinkle

Common Sundial

Atlantic Modulus

Plicate Horn Shell

Florida Cerith

Muddy Cerith

Mitchell's Wentletrap

White Wentletrap

Angulate Wentletrap

Humphrey's Wentletrap

Brown-Banded Wentletrap

Dwarf Purple Sea Snail

Common Purple Sea Snail

Globe Purple Sea Snail

Fighting Conch

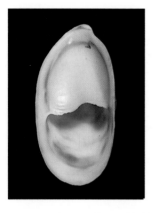

Common Atlantic Slipper Shell

Eastern White Slipper Shell

Atlantic Deer Cowrie

Sea Whip Simnia

Shark's Eye

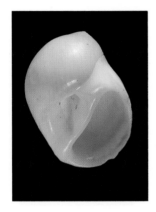

Brown Moon Shell

Colorful Atlantic Natica

Maculated Baby's Ear

Common Baby's Ear

Scotch Bonnet

Giant Tun Shell

Knobbed Triton

Gold-Mouthed Triton

Atlantic Hairy Triton

Poulsen's Triton

Von Salis' Triton

Atlantic Distorsio

Common Nutmeg

Common Atlantic Auger

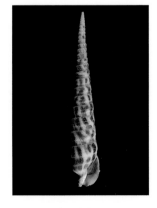

Flame Auger

Fine-Ribbed Auger

Marylee's Terebra

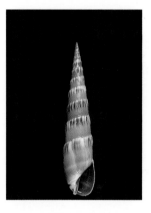

Sallé's Auger

Cancellate Cantharus

Tinted Cantharus

Common Eastern Nassa

Banded Tulip Shell

True Tulip Shell

Florida Horse Conch

Semiplicate Dove Shell

Lunar Dove Shell

Giant Eastern Murex

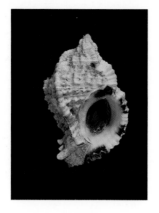

Apple Murex

Florida Rock Shell

Lettered Olive

Whitened Dwarf Olive

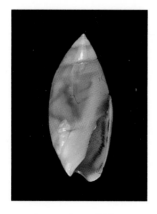

Minute Dwarf Olive

Common Atlantic Marginella

Striate Bubble

Coffee Melampus

Striped False Limpet

Mossy Ark

Turkey Wing

White Miniature Ark

Doc Bales' Ark

Incongruous Ark

Cut-Ribbed Ark

Blood Ark

Ponderous Ark

Hooked Mussel

Tulip Mussel

Ribbed Mussel

Paper Mussel

Half-Naked Pen Shell

Saw-Tooth Pen Shell

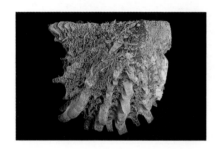

Atlantic Pearl Oyster

Atlantic Wing Oyster

Rough Scallop

Calico Scallop

Lion's Paw

Atlantic Thorny Oyster

Atlantic Thorny Oyster
(beach specimen)

Common Jingle Shell

Spiny Lima

Eastern Oyster

Thick Lucina

Tiger Lucina

Buttercup Lucina

Florida Lucina

True Spiny Jewel Box

Broad-Ribbed Cardita

Prickly Cockle

Yellow Cockle

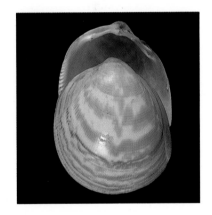

Common Egg Cockle

Morton's Egg Cockle

Giant Atlantic Cockle

Fragile Atlantic Mactra

Common Rangia

Atlantic Surf Clam

Smooth Duck Clam

Channeled Duck Clam

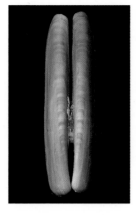

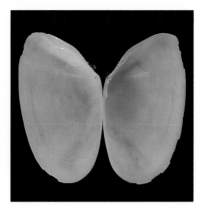

Jackknife Clam

DeKay's Dwarf Tellin

Alternate Tellin

White Crested Tellin

Constricted Macoma

Atlantic Sanguin

Purplish Semele

Purplish Tagelus

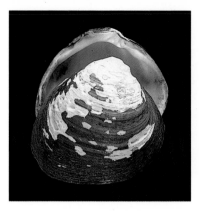

Carolina Marsh Clam

Calico Clam

Sunray Venus

Disk Dosinia

Elegant Dosinia

Cross-Barred Venus

Lady-in-Waiting Venus

Southern Quahog

Campeche Angel Wing

Angel Wing

Common Spirula

Sayella sp.

Genus *Peristichia* Dall, 1889
Peristichia toreta Dall, 1889

Size: 3 – 5 mm.
Color: Translucent grayish white alive; opaque white to brownish dead.
Shape: Ovate conic.
Ornament or sculpture: 4 to 6 convex whorls; suture fairly impressed; spiral sculpture absent or microscopic; nuclear whorls impressed in apex; may have chinklike umbilicus; quite variable.
Aperture: Ovate; columellar tooth weak.
Habitat: Ectoparasitic in inlet-influenced areas, shallow water; epifaunal.
Localities: Entire.
Occurrence: Fairly common in beach drift.
Range: Massachusetts to Texas.
Remarks: Species resembles *Odostomia laevigata* (Orbigny, 1842), which is primarily a West Indian species and does not range north to Massachusetts.

Size: 11 mm.
Color: White.
Shape: Elongate conic.
Ornament or sculpture: Spiral sculpture of 3 raised, rounded cords on upper whorls, 2 uppermost being nodulated, lower smooth; only 1 basal cord; columella without folds.
Aperture: Rounded.
Habitat: Shallow water.
Localities: Entire.
Occurrence: Uncommon in beach drift.
Range: North Carolina to western Florida; Texas.
Remarks: Usually placed with *Turbonillas* but now considered separate.

Genus *Eulimastoma* Bartsch, 1916

Eulimastoma cf. *E. canaliculata* (C.B. Adams, 1850)

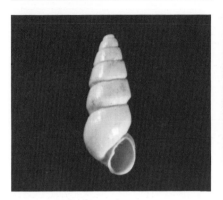

Size: 3.2 mm.
Color: White, smooth.
Shape: Conic, turreted.
Ornament or sculpture: Apex acute; spire with rectilinear outlines; 6 planulate whorls, with suture in small spiral channel; last whorl short, abruptly terminating.
Aperture: Broadly ovate, columellar plica nearly transverse.
Habitat: Offshore and inlet areas; epifaunal.
Localities: Entire.
Occurrence: Uncommon in beach drift.
Range: Texas; Jamaica.
Remarks: A most variable shell; [*Odostomia canaliculata*].

Eulimastoma cf. *E. harbisonae* Bartsch, 1955 [See *SST*, p. 174]

Eulimastoma cf. *E. teres* (Bush, 1885)

Size: 4.5 mm.
Color: White, lustrous.
Shape: Turreted.
Ornament or sculpture: About $7\frac{1}{2}$ flattened whorls, sutures canaliculate; whorls have distinct, impressed, spiral line just below angle; body whorl distinctly angulated at periphery where there is a prominent, rounded thread, with somewhat elongated, rounded base; nucleus large, very oblique.
Aperture: Not so much produced anteriorly; in juveniles plica very conspicuous; umbilicus small, deep, nearly concealed by reflected inner lip.
Habitat: Ectoparasitic in low-salinity bays; epifaunal.
Localities: Entire.
Occurrence: Fairly common in beach drift.
Range: Cape Hatteras; Texas.
Remarks: Suture variable; [*Odostomia teres*].

Weber's Eulimastoma
Eulimastoma cf. *E. weberi* (Morrison, 1965) [See *SST*, p. 175]

Genus *Turbonilla* Risso, 1826

According to Helmer Odé, author of a monograph in the *Texas Conchologist*, the genus *Turbonilla* may be restricted to the Atlantic Coast along New England. The shells depicted here were collected in Texas. They look similar to *Turbonilla* and *Chemitzia*. Use these IDs only as guides to locate these tiny shells.

Genus *Pyrgiscus* Philippi, 1841

Elegant Turbonilla
Pyrgiscus cf. *elegantula* Verrill, 1882

Size: 3–5 mm.
Color: Amber, semitransparent; spiral incisions darker.
Shape: Elongate conic, slender.
Ornament or sculpture: 9 rounded whorls; sutures distinct; 22 nearly perpendicular, rounded transverse ribs, separated by about equally wide spaces; spaces crossed by 5 equal, well-separated, incised spiral lines and 2 very much finer ones; rounded base incised with 9 unevenly spaced spiral lines.
Aperture: Elongated oval; columella nearly straight, slightly reflexed, with slight fold.
Habitat: Ectoparasitic, epifaunal.
Localities: Port Aransas.
Occurrence: Uncommon in beach drift.
Range: Texas; West Indies.
Remarks: Syn. *T. elegans* Verrill, 1872. *Belsa elegantula*, Verril, 1882.

Interrupted Turbonilla
Pyrgiscus cf. *interrupta* Totten, 1835

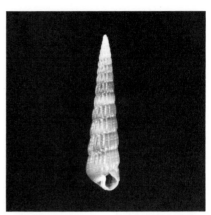

Size: 6 mm.
Color: Brownish.
Shape: Elongate conic, slender.
Ornament or sculpture: About 10 almost flat whorls sculptured with about 22 smooth, axial ribs separated by grooves of a little wider width, and with about 14 subequal, impressed, revolving lines arranged in pairs and entirely interrupted by ribs; spiral line above periphery heavier than others, forming line of deep pits; ribs obsolete below middle of body whorl; base short, rounded with spiral lines.
Aperture: Ovate, angular above, regularly rounded below, about one-fifth length of shell; outer lip sharp, slightly sinuous; columella slightly curved, weakly reflexed.
Habitat: Ectoparasitic in inlets and along shore; epifaunal.
Localities: Port Aransas, probably entire.
Occurrence: Fairly common.
Range: Maine to West Indies; Texas; Carmen, Campeche, Mexico; Gulf of Campeche; Yucatán; Brazil.
Remarks: Disappearance of original shell described by Totten has contributed to misinterpretation of this species.

75

Puerto Rican Turbonilla
Pyrgiscus cf. *portoricana* Dall &
Simpson, 1901

Hemphill's Turbonilla
Strioturbonilla cf. *hemphilli* Bush, 1899

Size: 4.7 mm.
Color: Translucent white with narrow
yellowish brown spiral band around
whorls about one-fourth breadth of
whorl above its suture; pale yellow
spiral band on middle of base.
Shape: Elongate conic.
Ornament or sculpture: 10 flattened
postnuclear whorls, slightly contracted
at sutures; whorls crossed with almost
vertical axial ribs, 16 on fifth and
increasing in number toward base;
intercostal spaces broad, wavy, wider
than ribs; base ribbed, crossed with 6
spiral striae.
Aperture: Subovate; columella oblique;
outer lip well rounded, meeting
columella at right angle; parietal callus
well defined; strong oblique fold near
insertion of columella; outer sculpture
visible through outer lip.
Habitat: Ectoparasitic in inlet areas;
epifaunal.
Localities: Port Aransas, south.
Occurrence: Uncommon in beach drift.
Range: Texas; West Indies.

Size: 10–12 mm.
Color: White.
Shape: Elongate conic, slender.
Ornament or sculpture: 12 postnuclear
whorls slightly convex, sculptured with
about 20 almost perpendicular
transverse ribs; rounded ribs separated
by about equally wide, deep, concave
spaces ending at periphery of body
whorl in clean-cut ends; base rounded,
smooth; entire surface covered with
microscopic striations.
Aperture: Squarish, somewhat
expanded below; inner lip thickened,
reflected.
Habitat: Ectoparasitic in inlet-
influenced areas; epifaunal.
Localities: Southern half of range,
probably entire.
Occurrence: Fairly common, in beach
drift.
Range: Western coast of Florida; Texas.

Subfamily CYCLOSTREMELLINAE
  D. Moore, 1966

Genus *Cyclostremella* Bush, 1897

Cyclostremella humilis (Bush, 1897)
  [See *SST*, p. 180]

Order ACTOPHILA Thiele, 1931
Superfamily ELLOBIACEA Adams,
  1855
Family ELLOBIIDAE Adams, 1855
Subfamily MELAMPINAE Stimpson,
  1851

Genus *Melampus* Montfort, 1810

Coffee Melampus
Melampus bidentatus Say, 1822

Size: 18 mm.
Color: Brown with cream-colored bands.
Shape: Ovate.
Ornament or sculpture: Rather thin shell smooth; about 5 whorls; spire low; body whorl predominates; omphalous.
Aperture: Nearly length of body whorl, expanded below; outer lip thin, curved into columella; columella short with 2 white plicae; internal lamellae inside body whorl.
Habitat: Under vegetation on bay and lagoon shores; epifaunal.
Localities: Entire.

Occurrence: Common.
Range: Florida to West Indies; Texas.
Remarks: Examination of stomachs of wild ducks shows this snail to be a favorite food; only breeds in water.

Subfamily PEDIPEDINAE Thiele, 1931

Genus *Pedipes* Bruguière, 1792

Stepping Shell
Pedipes mirabilis (Mühlfeld, 1818)

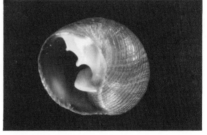

Size: 3–5 mm.
Color: Light to dark reddish brown.
Shape: Globose turbinate.
Ornament or sculpture: 4 to 5 strongly convex whorls; sculpture of numerous incised, spiral lines; transverse sculpture of irregular growth lines; spire slightly elevated; anomphalous.
Aperture: Oval with outer edge thin but thickened on inside; parietal area has 3 well-developed denticulations, top one being largest; outer lip has one tooth directly opposite central plica.
Habitat: Jetties and rocks above tide line; epifaunal.
Localities: Entire.
Occurrence: Uncommon.

Range: Bermuda; Florida to West Indies; Texas; Costa Rica; northeastern Brazil.
Remarks: This air breather can withstand environmental changes, but entire colony disappears under extreme conditions; prefers hard substratum.

Order HYGROPHILA Férussac, 1821
Superfamily SIPHONARIACEA Gray, 1840
Family SIPHONARIIDAE Gray, 1840

Genus *Siphonaria* Sowerby, 1824

Striped False Limpet
Siphonaria pectinata (Linné, 1758)

Size: 25.6 mm.
Color: Whitish with numerous brown bifurcating lines.
Shape: Conic, limpet-shaped.

Ornament or sculpture: Sculpture of numerous fine radial threads.
Aperture: Large, circular; interior glossy.
Habitat: Rocks and jetties; epifaunal.
Localities: Entire.
Occurrence: Common.
Range: Georgia; eastern Florida; Texas; Mexico; West Indies.
Remarks: Common on jetties of Texas coast; resembles true limpet, but animal air breather.

Order THECOSOMATA Blainville, 1824
Suborder EUTHECOSOMATA Meisenheimer, 1905
Superfamily SPIRATELLACEA Thiele, 1926
Family CUVIERIDAE Gray, 1840

Genus *Creseis* Rang, 1828

Straight-Needle Pteropod
Creseis acicula (Rang, 1828)

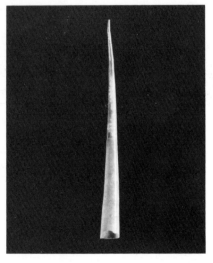

Size: 20–30 mm.
Color: White, translucent.
Shape: Elongated, straight cone.
Ornament or sculpture: Smooth, not coiled.

Aperture: Small, round.
Habitat: Pelagic, temperate and tropic seas.
Localities: Entire.
Occurrence: Common, seasonally, in beach drift.
Range: Worldwide.
Remarks: Looks like very fine tusk shell and easily overlooked; at times may come to shore by thousands.

Subfamily CAVOLINIINAE
   H. & A. Adams, 1854

Genus *Diacria* Gray, 1850

Four-Toothed Cavoline
Diacria quadridentata (Blainville, 1821)
   [See *SST*, p. 183]

Three-Spined Cavoline
Diacria trispinosa Blainville, 1821

Ornament or sculpture: Shell somewhat compressed with 3 straight spines, one on either side of aperture and longer one behind that may or may not be broken off; longitudinally ribbed on ventral side.
Aperture: Compressed, thickened; under lip curved outward.
Habitat: Pelagic, temperate and tropical seas.
Localities: Entire.
Occurrence: Uncommon in beach drift.
Range: Atlantic; Gulf of Mexico.
Remarks: Tends to rid itself of long hind stalk that would hamper swimming; descends during day, rises at night to feed; both sides of Panama.

Genus *Cavolina* Abildgaard, 1791

Long-Snout Cavoline
Cavolina longirostris (Blainville, 1821)

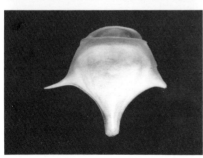

Size: 10 mm.
Color: Whitish with chestnut-colored lips.
Shape: Lozenge-shaped with extended hind part.

Size: 4–9 mm.
Color: Translucent white.
Shape: Triangular when viewed from top.

Ornament or sculpture: Ventral face of shell nearly round, sculptured with faint concentric ridges; dorsal face longitudinally ribbed, extended in front into long, slightly folded, depressed bead; lateral spines compressed; central spine short, truncated.
Aperture: Compressed, continued as fissure around side of shell.
Habitat: Pelagic, warm and tropical seas.
Localities: Entire.
Occurrence: Common in beach drift.
Range: Worldwide.
Remarks: Easily overlooked in beach drift because does not resemble usual concept of sea shell.

concentric ridges in front; dorsal face with 3 low, radiating ribs, turned downward and nearly evenly rounded at aperture; lateral spines compressed and curved backward; central spine short, stout, upcurved.
Aperture: Compressed, continued as fissure around each side of shell.
Habitat: Pelagic, warm and tropical seas.
Localities: Entire.
Occurrence: Fairly common in beach drift.
Range: Worldwide.

Uncinate Cavoline
Cavolina uncinata (Rang, 1829)

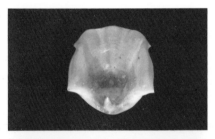

Size: 6–11 mm.
Color: Pale amber, translucent.
Shape: Shield-shaped when viewed from top.
Ornament or sculpture: Shell very inflated ventrally, surface delicately and regularly reticulated with fine,

Class BIVALVIA Linné, 1758 = [PELECYPODA Goldfuss, 1820]

Subclass PALAEOTAXODONTA
  Korobkov, 1954
Order NUCULOIDEA Dall, 1889
Superfamily NUCULACEA Gray, 1824
Family NUCULIDAE Gray, 1824

Genus *Nucula* Lamarck, 1799

Atlantic Nut Clam
Nucula cf. *N. proxima* Say, 1822

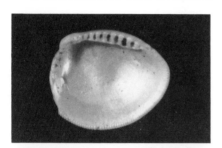

Size: 6.5 mm.
Color: Whitish.
Shape: Obliquely trigonal; equivalve; inequilateral.
Ornament or sculpture: Sculpture of faint growth lines and light radiating striae; margins rounded; ventral margin crenate.
Hinge area: Angular with 12 comblike teeth anterior to umbones and 18 posterior.
Pallial line & interior: Inner surface pearly; adductor muscle scars but no pallial sinus.
Habitat: Sandy mud bottom; infaunal.

Localities: East, central.
Occurrence: Fairly common in beach drift.
Range: Bermuda; Nova Scotia to Florida; Texas.
Remarks: Parker (in litt.) reports this clam common in Brazos River area.

Superfamily NUCULANACEA
  H. & A. Adams, 1858
Family NUCULANIDAE
  H. & A. Adams, 1858

Genus *Nuculana* Link, 1807

Pointed Nut Clam
Nuculana acuta (Conrad, 1831)

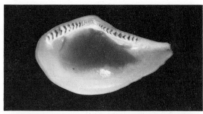

Size: 10 mm.
Color: White.
Shape: Elongate with pointed posterior rostrum; equivalve; inequilateral.
Ornament or sculpture: Sculpture of well-defined concentric grooves that do not extend over ridge on rostrum.

Hinge area: Small triangular chondrophore and numerous chevron-shaped teeth on either side of umbo.
Pallial line & interior: Interior polished; pallial sinus small, rounded.
Habitat: Sandy mud beyond low tide; infaunal.
Localities: Entire.
Occurrence: Fairly common in beach drift.
Range: Cape Cod to West Indies; Texas; Carmen, Campeche, Mexico; Gulf of Campeche; Campeche Bank.
Remarks: More common in southern part of state; less obese than *N. concentrica*; very variable; some may lack concentric sculpture.

Concentric Nut Clam
Nuculana concentrica Say, 1824

concentric growth lines on ventral half of valves; beaks and area just below smooth; radial ridge on rostrum smooth, not crossed by strong threads.
Hinge area: Numerous chevron-shaped teeth on either side of umbo.
Pallial line & interior: Pallial sinus small, rounded; polished.
Habitat: Sandy bottoms beyond low tide; infaunal.
Localities: Entire.
Occurrence: Fairly common in beach drift.
Range: Northwestern Florida to Texas; Surinam.
Remarks: More common in eastern part of state.

Subclass PTERIOMORPHIA Beurlen, 1944
Order ARCOIDEA Stoliczka, 1871
Superfamily ARCACEA Lamarck, 1809
Family ARCIDAE Lamarck, 1809
Subfamily ARCINAE Lamarck, 1809

Genus *Arca* Linné, 1758
Subgenus *Arca* s.s.

Mossy Ark
Arca (Arca) imbricata Bruguière, 1789

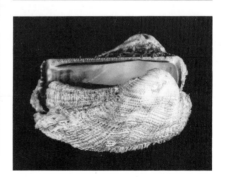

Size: 12–18 mm.
Color: Yellow white, semiglossy.
Shape: Rather obese and moderately rostrate; equivalve; inequilateral.
Ornament or sculpture: Adult shells appear smooth; have very fine,

Size: 25–38 mm.
Color: Whitish, concentrically marked with chestnut brown.
Shape: Rectangular; hinge long, straight; equivalve; inequilateral.
Ornament or sculpture: Numerous fine, irregular ribs crossed with growth lines giving a beaded appearance; posteriorly carinate; large ventral byssal gape.
Hinge area: Wide, flat; pear-shaped ligamental area between umbones; hinge margin straight with many small transverse teeth.
Pallial line & interior: Interior smooth, dull purplish; muscle scars connected by simple pallial line.
Habitat: On rocks or firm substratum; byssate epifaunal nestler.
Localities: Entire.
Occurrence: Common.
Range: North Carolina; Florida to West Indies; Texas; Campeche Bank; Costa Rica; Surinam; Brazil.
Remarks: Attaches with byssal threads; barely discernible unless movement of valves closing is seen; syn.
A. umbonata Lamarck, 1819.

Turkey Wing
Arca (Arca) zebra (Swainson, 1833)
 [See *SST*, p. 187]

Genus *Barbatia* Gray, 1847
Subgenus *Barbatia* s.s.

Red Brown Ark
Barbatia (Barbatia) cancellaria
(Lamarck, 1819) [See *SST*, p. 188]

White Bearded Ark
Barbatia (Barbatia) candida (Helbling, 1779)

Size: 25.4–50.8 mm.
Color: White.
Shape: Obliquely rectangular; hinge straight; equivalve; inequilateral.
Ornament or sculpture: Margins irregular; slight byssal gape on ventral edge; relatively thin for ark; numerous weak, slightly beaded ribs, those on posterior dorsal area being very strongly beaded; surface irregular.
Hinge area: Straight with narrow, lanceolate ligamental area between umbones, narrower than *Arca*; teeth not parallel, obliquely inclined to center.
Pallial line & interior: Interior white, smooth; pallial line simple with 2 muscle scars.
Habitat: On rocks beyond low tide; byssate epifaunal nestler.
Localities: Port Aransas, south.
Occurrence: Rare.
Range: North Carolina to West Indies; Texas; Brazil.
Remarks: Very few hinge teeth for ark; figure in *SST*, p. 188, is incorrect.

Subgenus *Acar* Gray, 1857

White Miniature Ark
Barbatia (Acar) domingensis (Lamarck, 1819)

Subgenus *Fugleria* Reinhart, 1937

Doc Bales' Ark
Barbatia (Fugleria) tenera (C.B.Adams, 1845)

Size: 12–18 mm.
Color: White to cream.
Shape: Rectangular; surface irregular; equivalve; inequilateral.
Ornament or sculpture: Very distinctive, coarsely reticulated surface; shinglelike growth ridges.
Hinge area: Ligament long, narrow, posterior to beaks; chevron-shaped teeth; umbo curled to edge of hinge.
Pallial line & interior: Pallial line simple with 2 muscle scars.
Habitat: On rocks below low tide; semi-epifaunal.
Localities: Southern half of coast.
Occurrence: Common.
Range: North Carolina to Florida; Texas; Gulf of Mexico to Quintana Roo; Costa Rica; Lesser Antilles; Surinam; Brazil; Brazilian oceanic islands.
Remarks: Look in holes and crevices of rocks on jetties.

Size: 25–38 mm.
Color: White.
Shape: Trapezoidal, rather fat; equivalve; nearly equilateral.
Ornament or sculpture: Thin shelled; numerous rather evenly, finely beaded, cordlike ribs, stronger posteriorly; small byssal gape.
Hinge area: Ligamental area fairly wide at umbo, narrowing anteriorly; typical chevron teeth.
Pallial line & interior: Interior polished, white; pallial line simple with 2 muscle scars.
Habitat: Offshore; byssate epifaunal nestler.
Localities: Entire.
Occurrence: Uncommon in beach drift.
Range: Lake Worth, Florida, to Texas; Caribbean; northern coast of South America.
Remarks: Specimen figured in *SST*, p. 189, may be *B. candida*; immature forms easily confused.

Subfamily ANADARINAE Reinhart, 1935

Genus *Anadara* Gray, 1847
Subgenus *Cunearca* Dall, 1898

Incongruous Ark
Anadara (Cunearca) brasiliana
(Lamarck, 1819)

Size: 25–38 mm.
Color: White.
Shape: Trigonal; left valve overlaps right; inequivalve; inequilateral.
Ornament or sculpture: 26 to 28 radial ribs visible, stronger at margins.
Hinge area: Umbones well separated; ligament area wide, excavated; oblique, comblike teeth smaller toward center.
Pallial line & interior: Interior white, polished; ribs visible and stronger at margins; pallial line simple with 2 muscle scars.
Habitat: Offshore in shallow water; infaunal.
Localities: Entire.
Occurrence: Common.
Range: Southeastern United States; Texas; West Indies; Surinam; Brazil.
Remarks: Most common ark on Texas coast; attaches by byssus to *Nassarius acutus* in symbiotic relationship; syn. *A. incongrua* Say, 1822.

Chemnitz's Ark
Anadara (Cunearca) chemnitzi
(Philippi, 1851)

Size: 25.6 mm.
Color: White.
Shape: Trigonal; inequivalve; inequilateral.
Ornament or sculpture: 26 to 28 broad ribs, strongly recurved posteriorly, bearing barlike beads.
Hinge area: Umbones well separated, forward of center of ligamental area; comblike teeth smaller toward center.
Pallial line & interior: Interior white, polished; ribs visible; pallial line simple with 2 muscle scars.
Habitat: Offshore in shallow water; epifaunal.
Localities: Extreme south.
Occurrence: Uncommon in beach drift.
Range: Texas; Mexico; Greater Antilles to Brazil; Surinam.
Remarks: Adult similar to *A. brasiliana* but heavier and smaller; juveniles very different.

Subgenus *Setiarca* Olsson, 1961

Cut-Ribbed Ark
Anadara (Setiarca) floridana (Conrad, 1869)

Subgenus *Larkiania* Reinhart, 1935

Transverse Ark
Anadara (Larkiana) transversa (Say, 1822)

Size: 63.5–127 mm.
Color: White.
Shape: Obliquely rectangular; equivalve; inequilateral.
Ornament or sculpture: Very heavy shell; 35 square ribs, each marked with deep central groove that does not extend over umbones and is not present on more rounded posterior ribs.
Hinge area: Umbones incurved, flattened; hinge margin straight; numerous comblike teeth.
Pallial line & interior: Interior marked with delicate lines; margins crenulate; pallial line simple and 2 muscle scars well defined.
Habitat: Deeper water offshore; infaunal.
Localities: Central, south.
Occurrence: Uncommon to rare beach shell.
Range: Southeastern United States; Texas; Greater Antilles.
Remarks: Line down center of rib makes this large ark distinctive and separates it (somewhat doubtfully) from *A. baughmani* Hertlein, 1951, a species from farther offshore; formerly referred to as *A. secticostata* Reeve, 1844, which has a brown stain; *A. lienosa* Say, 1822, a similar fossil form.

Size: 12–36 mm.
Color: White.
Shape: Transversely oblong; left valve overlaps right; equivalve; inequilateral.
Ornament or sculpture: 30 to 35 rounded ribs per valve; ribs on left valve usually beaded, seldom so on right valve.
Hinge area: Long, narrow ligamental space separates umbones; numerous teeth perpendicular to hinge line.
Pallial line & interior: Interior polished; pallial line simple with 2 muscle scars.
Habitat: Littoral to 10.8 meters (6 fathoms); inlet-influenced areas and offshore; infaunal.
Localities: Entire.
Occurrence: Common.
Range: South of Cape Cod to Florida; Texas to Carmen, Campeche, Mexico; Gulf of Campeche.
Remarks: Highly variable.

Subgenus *Lunarca* Reinhart, 1943
Blood Ark
Anadara (Lunarca) ovalis (Bruguière, 1789)

Size: 38–59 mm.
Color: White.
Shape: Roundish to ovate; equivalve; inequilateral.
Ornament or sculpture: Ribs have weak groove in center; strong intercostal ribs; left valve more heavily sculptured than right; no byssal gape.
Hinge area: Ligament very narrow; umbones close together; comblike teeth.
Pallial line & interior: Pallial line simple with 2 muscle scars; ribs visible on polished white interior.
Habitat: Just offshore; infaunal.
Localities: Entire.
Occurrence: Common.
Range: Cape Cod to West Indies; Gulf states; Costa Rica; Brazilian coast to Rocha, Uruguay.
Remarks: Animal bright red; syn. *A. campechiensis* Gmelin, 1791.

Family NOETIIDAE Stewart, 1930
Subfamily NOETIINAE Stewart, 1930

Genus *Noetia* Gray, 1840
Subgenus *Eontia* MacNeil, 1938

Ponderous Ark
Noetia (Eontia) ponderosa (Say, 1822)

Size: 50.8–63.5 mm.
Color: White.
Shape: Trigonal; equivalve; inequilateral.
Ornament or sculpture: Heavy, thick shell; 32 flattened square ribs with fine line down center; posterior margin nearly straight, keeled; fine concentric intercostal sculpture absent from umbones.
Hinge area: Umbones well separated; sides of hinge area slope obliquely downward to straight margin; teeth comblike.
Pallial line & interior: Pallial line simple with 2 strong, raised muscle scars; no byssal threads in adults.
Habitat: Inlet areas and offshore on sandy bottom; infaunal.
Localities: Entire.
Occurrence: Common.
Range: Virginia to Key West; Gulf of Mexico.

Order MYTILOIDEA Férussac, 1822
Superfamily MYTILACEA Rafinesque,
   1815
Family MYTILIDAE Rafinesque, 1815
Subfamily MYTILINAE Rafinesque,
   1815

Genus *Brachidontes* Swainson, 1840
Subgenus *Brachidontes* s.s.

Scorched Mussel
Brachidontes (Brachidontes) exustus
   (Linné, 1758)

Size: 18–38 mm.
Color: Yellowish brown to dark
brown; interior metallic purple and
white.
Shape: Moderately fan-shaped.
Ornament or sculpture: Numerous
rounded, radial ribs dividing near ventral margin and eroded near umbones;
slight byssal gape in ventral margin.
Hinge area: 2 small teeth at anterior
end; 5 to 6 tiny teeth on edge of shell at
posterior end, beyond ligament.
Pallial line & interior: Pallial line weak,
simple; posterior muscle scar larger
than anterior.
Habitat: On rocks or oyster reefs in
bays and inlets; byssate closely attached
epifaunal.
Localities: Entire.
Occurrence: Common.
Range: North Carolina to West Indies;
Texas; Yucatán; Quintana Roo;
Brazilian coast to Uruguay.
Remarks: Attaches by byssus to jetties
and oyster reefs; not in brackish water
in Texas; often confused with
B. citrinus, Röding, 1798, which is
larger and has 4 anterior teeth.

Genus *Ischadium* Jukes-Brown, 1905

Hooked Mussel
Ischadium recurvum (Rafinesque, 1820)

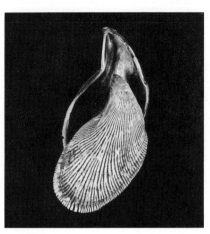

Size: 25.6–63.5 mm.
Color: Purplish gray.
Shape: Oval with strong triangular
hook on anterior end.
Ornament or sculpture: Strong radial,
rounded ribs dividing near ventral
margin; microscopic growth lines cross
ribs.
Hinge area: Umbones at end of hook;
3 or 4 small teeth near umbones;
ligament strong, in large groove
extending from umbones to peak of
dorsal margin.
Pallial line & interior: Interior shiny
purple, reddish brown, nacreous;
pallial line simple with 1 large posterior
muscle scar.
Habitat: Oyster reef in low-salinity
bays; byssate closely attached
epifaunal.
Localities: Entire.
Occurrence: Common.
Range: Cape Cod to West Indies;
Texas; Carmen, Campeche, Mexico;
Gulf of Campeche.
Remarks: Lives on low-salinity reefs of
Crassostrea virginica (Gmelin, 1792);
during periods of drought *Brachidontes
exustus* and *Ostrea equestris* Say, 1834,
will completely replace *I. recurvum* and
C. virginica.

Subfamily CRENELLINAE Adams & Adams, 1857

Genus *Gregariella* Monterosato, 1884

Common Gregariella
Gregariella coralliophaga (Gmelin, 1791)

Genus *Lioberis* Dall, 1898

Say's Chestnut Mussel
Lioberis castaneus (Say, 1822)

Size: 17 mm.
Color: Reddish brown; interior iridescent.
Shape: Oval.
Ornament or sculpture: Smooth except for growth lines; posterior dorsal area somewhat keeled.
Hinge area: Weak, tiny denticulations along hinge.
Pallial line & interior: Pallial line simple; inner edges finely serrate.
Habitat: Bores into rock and coral offshore; semi-infaunal.
Localities: Entire.
Occurrence: Fairly common.
Range: Cape Hatteras to Brazil; Gulf of Mexico; Yucatán.
Remarks: Weaves nest of byssal threads; [*Musculus opifex*]; syn. *G. opifex* (Say, 1815).

Size: 25 mm.
Color: Bluish white.
Shape: Elongate oval, inflated.
Ornament or sculpture: Smooth except for fine, concentric growth lines.
Hinge area: Umbones slightly back from anterior end; no teeth.
Pallial line & interior: Interior smooth, nacreous; no marginal crenulation; pallial line simple.
Habitat: Open-bay margins, inlets, along shore; infaunal.
Localities: Central, south.
Occurrence: Uncommon in beach drift.
Range: South Carolina to Florida Keys and West Indies; Texas; Yucatán; Brazil.
Remarks: [*Botula castanea* (Say, 1822)].

Genus *Musculus* Röding, 1798
Subgenus *Ryenella* Fleming, 1959

Lateral Musculus
Musculus (Ryenella) lateralis (Say, 1822)

Size: 10 mm.
Color: Variable: light brown, pink, or greenish; interior iridescent.
Shape: Oblong.
Ornament or sculpture: Concentric growth lines over entire surface; radial ribs on either end leaving disc section with only finer growth lines.
Hinge area: Umbones not terminal; no teeth.
Pallial line & interior: Pallial line simple.
Habitat: Attached to tunicates; semi-infaunal.
Localities: Port Aransas, probably entire.
Occurrence: Uncommon.
Range: North Carolina to Florida; Texas; Yucatán; Quintana Roo; West Indies; Brazil.
Remarks: Look in colonies of tunicates (sea pork); attached by byssus.

Subfamily LITHOPHAGINAE Adams & Adams, 1857

Genus *Lithophaga* Röding, 1798
Subgenus *Diberus* Dall, 1898

Mahogany Date Mussel
Lithophaga (Diberus) bisulcata
  (Orbigny, 1845)

Size: 25–38 mm.
Color: Mahogany brown.
Shape: Elongate cylindrical, coming to point at one end.
Ornament or sculpture: Weak concentric growth lines; 2 oblique furrows going from dorsal margin to posterior; covered with gray calcareous deposits.
Hinge area: Umbones not terminal; no teeth.
Pallial line & interior: Anterior muscle in front of umbo.
Habitat: In rocks in both shallow and deep water; infaunal.
Localities: Entire.
Occurrence: Common.
Range: Bermuda; North Carolina to Florida; Texas; West Indies; Surinam; Brazil.
Remarks: Crush jetty rock carefully with hammer to recover these borers; their habit of boring into *Crassostrea virginica* may be of concern to persons cultivating oysters commercially.

Subgenus *Myoforceps* P. Fischer, 1886

Scissor Date Mussel

Lithophaga (Myoforceps) aristata
  (Dillwyn, 1817)

Subfamily MODIOLINAE Keen, 1958

Genus *Modiolus* Lamarck, 1799

Tulip Mussel

Modiolus americanus (Leach, 1815)

Size: 25–38 mm.
Color: Grayish white.
Shape: Cylindrical with one end pointed.
Ornament or sculpture: Smooth; points at posterior end that cross each other in scissor-fashion formed by calcareous deposit over periostracum.
Hinge area: Umbones not terminal; no teeth.
Pallial line & interior: Interior nacreous.
Habitat: In rocks in both shallow and deep water; infaunal.
Localities: Central, south.
Occurrence: Fairly common.
Range: North Carolina to Florida; Texas; Yucatán; West Indies; La Jolla, California, to Peru.
Remarks: Found in same manner as *L. bisulcata.*

Size: 25–101 mm.
Color: Light brown with blush of rose red and streaks of purple.
Shape: Trigonal.
Ornament or sculpture: Only fine growth lines.
Hinge area: Anterior margin without teeth; umbones away from end of shell; ligament in groove posterior to umbones.
Pallial line & interior: Pallial line weak, simple; posterior muscle scar larger than anterior.
Habitat: Offshore below low-water mark; byssate closely attached epifaunal.
Localities: Entire.
Occurrence: Fairly common beach shell.
Range: Bermuda; North Carolina to West Indies; Texas; Campeche Bank; Yucatán; Surinam; Brazilian coast to Bahia.
Remarks: Color intense red on Texas coast and purple in Florida; [*Volsella* or *Modiolus tulipa* Lamarck, 1819].

Genus *Amygdalum* Megerle von
 Muhlfeld, 1811

Paper Mussel
Amygdalum papyria (Conrad, 1846)

Genus *Geukensia* Poel, 1959

Ribbed Mussel
Geukensia demissa granosissima
 (G. B. Sowerby III, 1914)

Size: 25–38 mm.
Color: Exterior grayish; interior
iridescent, metallic white.
Shape: Elongate fan-shaped.
Ornament or sculpture: Very delicate
and fragile with only fine concentric
growth lines.
Hinge area: Umbones slightly beyond
anterior end; ligament weak and thin;
no teeth.
Pallial line & interior: Pallial line
simple and muscle scar faint.
Habitat: Open bays and inlet-
influenced areas; semi-infaunal.
Localities: Entire.
Occurrence: Fairly common.
Range: Maryland to Florida; Texas.
Remarks: Carefully dig for these
nestlers around roots of marine grass.

Size: 50.8–101 mm.
Color: Brown, shiny.
Shape: Elongate trigonal with rounded
posterior margin.
Ornament or sculpture: Numerous
strong radial, beaded ribs dividing near
posterior margin.
Hinge area: Long, narrow; no teeth;
ligament in groove posterior to
umbones slightly away from end of
shell.
Pallial line & interior: Interior
nacreous; pallial line rather strong,
simple, with small muscle scar at
anterior end and larger one at upper
part of posterior end.
Habitat: Salt marshes; byssate closely
attached epifaunal.
Localities: East.
Occurrence: Common.
Range: Both sides of Florida; Gulf
states; Yucatán.
Remarks: Imbeds in roots of marsh
grass; referred to as *Modiola demissus*
(Dillwyn, 1817).

Superfamily PINNACEA Leach, 1819
Family PINNIDAE Leach, 1819

Genus *Atrina* Gray, 1840
Half-Naked Pen Shell
Atrina seminuda (Lamarck, 1819)

Size: 235–250 mm.
Color: Translucent, grayish tan sometimes mottled with purple brown.
Shape: Wedge-shaped.
Ornament or sculpture: Spinose, radiating ribs with ventral slope usually smooth; ribs often smooth; growth lines fine.
Hinge area: Longest dimension of shell, straight; no teeth.
Pallial line & interior: Nacreous area about one-half to two-thirds length of shell; small posterior adductor muscle scar well within nacreous area, never protruding beyond it; anterior adductor scar small, nearly as wide as anterior end of shell, separates this shell from *A. rigida*; pallial line simple.
Habitat: Offshore and in inlet-influenced bays; semi-infaunal.
Localities: Entire.
Occurrence: Fairly common.
Range: Eastern United States; Texas; Yucatán; Surinam; Brazil to Argentina.

Remarks: Lives in colonies in mud attached with byssal threads; only posterior margin above substratum; margin of mantle yellow, foot lighter yellow; adductor muscle edible; less common than *A. serrata*; a small crab commensal with and lives within pen shell.

Saw-Tooth Pen Shell
Atrina serrata (G. B. Sowerby I, 1825)

Size: Up to 250 mm.
Color: Translucent light tan to medium greenish brown.
Shape: Wedge-shaped; thin, fragile, shiny.
Ornament or sculpture: Uniform sculpture of about 30 low ribs covered with fluted projections; sculpture much finer on ventral slope.
Hinge area: Straight to slightly concave without teeth.
Pallial line & interior: Interior has nacreous layer usually covering three-fourths length of valve; posterior adductor muscle scar nearly circular, set well within nacreous layer; anterior scar small; pallial line simple.
Habitat: Offshore in inner shelf zone; semi-infaunal.
Localities: Entire.
Occurrence: Common.

Range: North Carolina to West Indies; Texas; Surinam.
Remarks: Much thinner and spines more tubular than *A. seminuda*; nacreous area larger; at times washed up on Gulf beaches by hundreds; adductor muscle may be prepared to eat in same way as scallops; harvested in Mexico for canning as scallops; pair of colorless shrimp live commensally with *A. serrata*.

Order PTERIOIDEA Newell, 1965
Suborder PTERIINA Newell, 1965
Superfamily PTERIACEA Gray, 1847
Family PTERIIDAE Gray, 1847

Genus *Pinctada* Röding, 1798

Atlantic Pearl Oyster
Pinctada imbricata Röding, 1798

Size: 38–76 mm.
Color: Variable: purplish brown or black.
Shape: Roundish with 2 short wings; inequivalve; inequilateral.
Ornament or sculpture: Flat with concentrically arranged scaly projections of periostracum; byssal gape under anterior wing of right valve.
Hinge area: Straight with single lateral tooth in left valve, double laterals in right.

Pallial line & interior: Interior very nacreous with wide polished border around margins; pallial line simple.
Habitat: Offshore attached to rock or gorgonia, a soft coral; byssate free-swinging epifaunal.
Localities: Southern half of coast.
Occurrence: Uncommon to rare beach shell.
Range: Southern half of Florida; Texas; Gulf of Mexico to Quintana Roo; West Indies; Brazil.
Remarks: Adults seldom found; forms beautiful pearls; syn. *P. radiata* Leach, 1819.

Genus *Pteria* Scopoli, 1777

Atlantic Wing Oyster
Pteria colymbus (Röding, 1798)

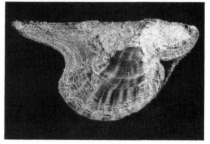

Size: 38–76 mm.
Color: Brownish black with broken, radial lines of cream color; interior highly nacreous.
Shape: Oval with posterior drawn-out wing; inequivalve; inequilateral.
Ornament or sculpture: Smooth surface; byssal gape near anterior wing.
Hinge area: Straight with elongated posterior ear, or wing; 2 small cardinal teeth and 1 lateral tooth in each valve.
Pallial line & interior: Interior nacreous with single, almost central muscle scar; pallial line simple.
Habitat: Offshore reefs and on "whistling buoy" out of Port Aransas attached to alcyonarians; byssate free-swinging epifaunal.

Localities: Southern two-thirds of coast.
Occurrence: Uncommon beach shell.
Range: Bermuda; southeastern United States; Texas; Costa Rica; West Indies; Brazil.
Remarks: Washes in attached to gorgonia.

Family ISOGNOMONIDAE Woodring, 1925

Genus *Isognomon* Lightfoot, 1786

Flat Tree Oyster
Isognomon alatus (Gmelin, 1791)

Size: 50.8–76 mm.
Color: Drab, dirty gray; interior nacreous, purplish.
Shape: Flat, fan-shaped.
Ornament or sculpture: Rough with flaky lamellations.
Hinge area: Straight with 8 to 12 oblong grooves; byssal gape on anterior margin near dorsal margin.
Pallial line & interior: Pallial line simple, discontinuous.
Habitat: In crevices on jetties; byssate free-swinging epifaunal.
Localities: Port Aransas, south.
Occurrence: Uncommon.
Range: Bermuda; southern half of Florida; Texas; southern Mexico; Campeche Bank; Central America; West Indies; Brazilian oceanic islands.
Remarks: Look carefully on jetties; very undistinguished appearance.

Two-Toned Tree Oyster
Isognomon bicolor (C.B. Adams, 1845)

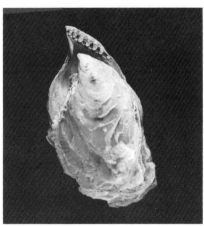

Size: 12–50 mm.
Color: Yellowish with purple splotches; variable.
Shape: Very irregular, elongated parallelogram.
Ornament or sculpture: Rough with flaky lamellations.
Hinge area: Short, straight, with 4 to 8 small, square sockets; anterior byssal gape near dorsal margin.
Pallial line & interior: Sharply raised ridge separates central area from marginal area; color of interior frequently different on opposite sides of ridge; pallial line simple, discontinuous.
Habitat: In clusters on rocks in inlet-influenced areas; byssate free-swinging epifaunal.
Localities: Port Aransas, south.
Occurrence: Uncommon.
Range: Bermuda; Florida Keys; Texas; southern Mexico; Campeche Bank; Yucatán; Costa Rica; Caribbean.
Remarks: More common than *I. alatus.*

Superfamily PECTINACEA Rafinesque, 1815
Family PECTINIDAE Rafinesque, 1815
Subfamily CHLAMYDINAE Korobkov, 1960

Genus *Aequipecten* P. Fischer, 1886

Rough Scallop
Aequipecten muscosus (W. Wood, 1818) [See *SST*, p. 201]

Genus *Argopecten* Monterosato, 1899

Calico Scallop
Argopecten gibbus (Linné, 1758) [See *SST*, p. 202]

Atlantic Bay Scallop
Argopecten irradians amplicostatus (Dall, 1898)

Size: 50.8–76 mm.
Color: Upper valve mottled gray and white.
Shape: Fan-shaped, almost circular.
Ornament or sculpture: 12 to 17 high, squarish ribs; rather inflated.
Hinge area: Straight; no teeth; ears not as wide as shell.
Pallial line & interior: Single muscle scar; pallial line simple.
Habitat: Bays, open lagoons; free-living epifaunal.
Localities: Entire.
Occurrence: Common.
Range: Central Texas to Tuxpan, Veracruz, Mexico.
Remarks: Lives in bays; often washed up by hundreds after norther; worn valves on outer beaches orange or black; in aquarium "eyes" of this active bivalve visible around mantle edge; juvenile attaches to rock by byssus; when pulled off will reattach itself; will "flap" valves and skip about tank; [*Aequipecten irradians amplicostatus*].

Genus *Lyropecten* Conrad, 1862
Subgenus *Nodipecten* Dall, 1898

Lion's Paw
Lyropecten (Nodipecten) nodosus (Linné, 1758)

Size: 76–152 mm.
Color: Bright red, deep orange, or maroon red.
Shape: Fan-shaped; nearly equivalve; inequilateral.
Ornament or sculpture: 7 to 9 large, coarse ribs that have large, hollow nodules; also numerous cordlike riblets.
Hinge area: Straight; no teeth.
Pallial line & interior: Pallial line simple with single large muscle scar.
Habitat: Offshore; epifaunal fissure dweller.
Localities: South.
Occurrence: Uncommon to rare.
Range: Florida Keys; Texas; Mexico; West Indies; Surinam; Brazil.
Remarks: Halves of shell found, rarely, on southern part of coast; living specimens found by divers on 7½ Fathom Reef and other offshore banks.

Subfamily PECTININAE Rafinesque, 1815

Genus *Pecten* Müller, 1776
Subgenus *Euvola* Dall, 1898

Ravenel's Scallop
Pecten (Euvola) raveneli Dall, 1898 [See *SST*, p. 203]

Family PLICATULIDAE Watson, 1930

Genus *Plicatula* Lamarck, 1801

Kitten's Paw
Plicatula gibbosa Lamarck, 1801

Size: 25 mm.
Color: Whitish with red brown lines on ribs.
Shape: Fan-shaped; inequivalve.
Ornament or sculpture: Rather heavy with 5 to 7 raised ribs that crenulate margin so that valves interlock; attached by right valve.
Hinge area: 2 hinge teeth in each valve lock into corresponding notches in opposite valve, as in *Spondylus*; ligament internal.
Pallial line & interior: Pallial line simple.
Habitat: Offshore on banks; cemented epifaunal.
Localities: Entire.
Occurrence: Uncommon.
Range: Bermuda; North Carolina to Florida; Gulf states; Campeche Bank;

Yucatán; West Indies; Surinam; Brazil; Uruguay.
Remarks: Dead shells not uncommon on outer beaches and in spoil banks; look for it attached to pieces of offshore drilling rigs occasionally brought in; attaches by right valve.

Family SPONDYLIDAE Gray, 1826

Genus *Spondylus* Linné, 1758

Atlantic Thorny Oyster
Spondylus americanus Hermann, 1781

(beachworm *Spondylus*)

Size: 76–101 mm.
Color: Variable: white with orange or yellow umbones, rose or cream.
Shape: Nearly circular to oval; inequivalve.
Ornament or sculpture: Adults have spines up to 2 inches in length that are

97

erect, arranged radially; lower valve larger and deeper than upper.
Hinge area: 2 large cardinal teeth on either side of ligament in each valve align with sockets in opposite valve.
Pallial line & interior: Interior smooth and white with 1 large muscle scar; pallial line simple.
Habitat: Offshore attached to reefs; cemented epifaunal.
Localities: Southern half of coast.
Occurrence: Uncommon.
Range: North Carolina to Florida; Texas; Campeche Bank; Yucatán; Central America; West Indies; Brazil.
Remarks: Worn, faded valves found on Texas beaches bear little resemblance to spectacular living specimen brought up by divers offshore; ball-and-socket hinge distinguishes these eroded specimens from *Chama*.

near umbones from which chitinous byssus projects to anchor shell.
Hinge area: Ligament not supported with teeth or ridges.
Pallial line & interior: Interior nacreous; pallial line simple, not distinct; upper valve has large muscle scar opposite hole and 2 smaller ones below.
Habitat: Hypersaline oyster or rock reef; byssate closely attached epifaunal.
Localities: Entire.
Occurrence: Common.
Range: Bermuda; eastern United States; Gulf of Mexico; Gulf of Campeche; Quintana Roo; West Indies to Brazil; Surinam.
Remarks: Often attached to oyster or old shell; usually only top valve found in drift; some old specimens have turned black.

Superfamily ANOMIACEA Rafinesque, 1815
Family ANOMIIDAE Rafinesque, 1815

Genus *Anomia* Linné, 1758

Common Jingle Shell
Anomia simplex Orbigny, 1845

Genus *Pododesmus* Philippi, 1837

Rough Jingle Shell
Pododesmus rudis (Broderip, 1834)

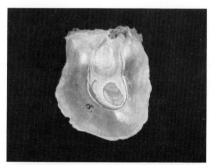

Size: 25 – 51 mm.
Color: Variable: translucent yellow or dull orange; shiny.
Shape: Subcircular; upper valve more convex than flat attached valve.
Ornament or sculpture: Wavy undulating sculpture; shape conforms to contours and texture of surface on which attached; lower valve has hole

Size: Up to 51 mm.
Color: Brownish; lower valve white.
Shape: Irregular; upper valve convex; lower valve flat with hole near umbones.
Ornament or sculpture: Rough, wavy surface arranged somewhat concentrically.
Hinge area: Narrow; no teeth.
Pallial line & interior: Muscle scar in top valve opposite hole with second large scar diagonally below it; pallial line simple.
Habitat: On rock in inlet-influenced areas; byssate closely attached epifaunal.
Localities: South.
Occurrence: Rare.
Range: Bermuda; South Carolina to Florida; Texas; Brazilian coast to Argentina.

Superfamily LIMACEA Rafinesque, 1815
Family LIMIDAE Rafinesque, 1815

Genus *Lima* Bruguière, 1797
Subgenus *Lima* s.s.

Spiny Lima
Lima (Lima) lima (Linné, 1758) [See *SST*, p. 206]

Subgenus *Limaria* Link, 1807

Antillean Lima
Lima (Limaria) pellucida C. B. Adams, 1846 [See *SST*, p. 206]

Suborder OSTREINA Férussac, 1822
Superfamily OSTREACEA Rafinesque, 1815
Family OSTREIDAE Rafinesque, 1815

Genus *Crassostrea* Sacco, 1897

Eastern Oyster
Crassostrea virginica (Gmelin, 1791)

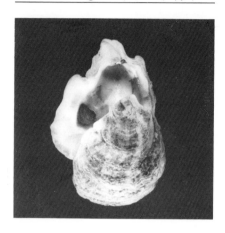

Size: 51–150 mm.
Color: Dull gray.
Shape: Very irregular and variable from oval to weirdly elongate.
Ornament or sculpture: Surface rough with leaflike scales; valve margins slightly undulating or straight; beaks long, curved; upper valve smaller, flatter, smoother than lower.
Hinge area: Shell attached at umbo of left valve, which is longer than that of right valve; both umbones have central channel for ligamentary attachment.
Pallial line & interior: Muscle scar subcentral, colored deep purple; interior smooth; pallial line simple.
Habitat: Brackish bays and estuaries; cemented epifaunal.
Localities: Entire.
Occurrence: Common.
Range: Gulf of St. Lawrence to Gulf of Mexico: Yucatán; West Indies.
Remarks: This commercially important bivalve discussed in Bulletin No. 40 of Texas Game and Fish Commission; does not have interior marginal teeth of *Ostrea equestris*.

Genus *Ostrea* Linné, 1758

Horse or Crested Oyster
Ostrea equestris Say, 1834

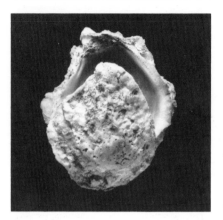

Size: 25–51 mm.
Color: Dull gray to brownish; interior gray green.
Shape: Rather oval, fairly constant shape.
Ornament or sculpture: Surface rough with raised, crenulated margins; left valve flatter than right; 6 to 12 teeth on larger valve with corresponding cavities on smaller valve.
Hinge area: Narrow, curved.
Pallial line & interior: Muscle centrally located; scar not pigmented; pallial line simple.
Habitat: High-salinity oyster reef; cemented epifaunal.
Localities: Entire.
Occurrence: Common.
Range: Southeastern United States; Gulf states; West Indies; Brazilian coast to Argentina.
Remarks: Economically important bivalve; requires more saline environment than *Crassostrea virginica* and will replace latter during sustained drought.

Subclass HETERODONTA Neumayr, 1884
Order VENEROIDEA H. & A. Adams, 1858
Suborder LUCININA Dall, 1889
Superfamily LUCINACEA Fleming, 1828
Family LUCINIDAE Fleming, 1828
Subfamily LUCININAE Fleming, 1828

Genus *Lucina* Bruguière, 1797

Thick Lucina
Lucina pectinata (Gmelin, 1791)

Size: 25–63 mm.
Color: Pale yellow to orange.
Shape: Oval, lenticular.
Ornament or sculpture: Posterior dorsal slope rostrate, anterior slope less rostrate; sculpture of unequally spaced lamellate ridges with finer lines in interspaces.
Hinge area: Ligament partially visible from outside; lunule small; anterior and posterior lateral teeth strong; cardinals weak.
Pallial line & interior: Pallial line simple with 2 muscle scars; anterior scar very elongate.
Habitat: In grass flats in open-bay margins and hypersaline lagoons; infaunal.
Localities: Entire.
Occurrence: Common.
Range: North Carolina to Florida;

Texas; Quintana Roo; West Indies;
Central America to Brazil.
Remarks: [*Phacoides pectinatus*].

Genus *Codakia* Scopoli, 1777
Subgenus *Codakia* s.s.

Tiger Lucina
Codakia (Codakia) orbicularis (Linné,
1758)

Size: 63–87 mm.
Color: White.
Shape: Orbicular, compressed;
equivalve.
Ornament or sculpture: Reticulate
sculpture of coarse radial lines crossed
by finer concentric threads.
Hinge area: Lunule in front of beaks
deep, heart-shaped, and nearly all on
right valve; right valve has 2 cardinal
teeth and 1 anterior lateral close to
them; left valve has 2 cardinals, large
double anterior lateral, and small
double posterior lateral.
Pallial line & interior: Pallial line
simple with 2 muscle scars.
Habitat: Shallow interreef flats in sand;
infaunal.
Localities: Port Aransas, south.
Occurrence: Rare beach shell.
Range: Bermuda; Florida; Texas;
Campeche Bank; Yucatán; Costa Rica;
northeastern and eastern Brazil.
Remarks: Only specimens found very
chalky and worn halves, probably
Pleistocene fossils.

Genus *Linga* De Gregorio, 1884
Subgenus *Bellucina* Dall, 1901

Lovely Miniature Lucina
[*Linga (Bellucina) amianta* (Dall, 1901)]

Size: 6–10 mm.
Color: White.
Shape: Orbicular; equivalve;
subequilateral.
Ornament or sculpture: Rather inflated,
thickened shell; sculptured with 8 to 9
wide, rounded ribs crossed by
numerous, small concentric threads.
Hinge area: Umbones touching; lunule
small; cardinal teeth small, not visible
in adults; laterals well developed in
right valve with sockets in left.
Pallial line & interior: Pallial line
simple with 2 muscle scars; margin
crenulate.
Habitat: Inlet-influenced areas and near
shore; infaunal.
Localities: Entire.
Occurrence: Common in beach drift.
Range: North Carolina to both sides of
Florida; Texas; northeastern and
eastern Brazil.
Remarks: More abundant in eastern
part of Texas coast; [*Lucina amiantus*].

Genus *Parvilucina* Dall, 1901

Many-Lined Lucina
Parvilucina multilineata (Holmes, 1859)

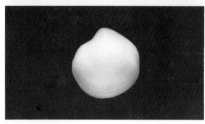

Size: 6–10 mm.
Color: White.
Shape: Orbicular; equivalve.
Ornament or sculpture: Sculpture of numerous, fine, concentric threads stronger near umbones.
Hinge area: Small cardinal and lateral teeth in right and left valves; umbones small.
Pallial line & interior: Pallial line simple with 2 muscle scars; interior margin finely crenulate.
Habitat: Offshore and inlet-influenced areas; infaunal.
Localities: Entire.
Occurrence: Common in beach drift.
Range: North Carolina to both sides of Florida; Texas; Yucatán; Quintana Roo; eastern and southern Brazil.
Remarks: More common to south; [*Lucina multilineata*]; syn. *Linga crenella* Dall, 1901.

Subfamily MILTHINAE Chavan, 1969

Genus *Anodontia* Link, 1807

Buttercup Lucina
Anodontia alba Link, 1807

Size: 38–51 mm.
Color: Exterior white; interior flushed with yellowish orange.
Shape: Oval or circular, inflated; equivalve.
Ornament or sculpture: Sculpture of weak, irregular concentric growth lines.
Hinge area: Hinge with weak teeth; umbones not prominent; hinge extended anteriorly to faint oval lunule.
Pallial line & interior: Pallial line simple with 2 muscle scars; anterior scar elongate, nearly parallel to pallial line; margins smooth.
Habitat: Inlet-influenced areas, bay margins, hypersaline lagoons; infaunal.
Localities: Entire.
Occurrence: Fairly common beach shell.
Range: Bermuda; North Carolina to Florida; Gulf states; Campeche Bank; Yucatán; Costa Rica; West Indies.
Remarks: Unusual on northern half of Texas coast.

Chalky Buttercup
Anodontia philippiana (Reeve, 1850)

Genus *Pseudomiltha* P. Fischer, 1885
Florida Lucina
Pseudomiltha floridana (Conrad, 1833)

Size: 51–101 mm.
Color: Chalky white.
Shape: Orbicular, inflated; equivalve.
Ornament or sculpture: Fine concentric growth lines; interior usually pustulose.
Hinge area: Umbones rounded and touching; hinge with very weak teeth.
Pallial line & interior: Pallial line simple with 2 muscle scars; anterior scar juts away from line at 30° angle instead of being parallel as in *A. alba.*
Habitat: Offshore at moderate depths; infaunal.
Localities: Port Aransas, south.
Occurrence: Uncommon beach shell.
Range: Bermuda; North Carolina to eastern Florida; Texas; Cuba.
Remarks: May be same as *A. schrammi* (Crosse, 1876); no longer living on Texas coast; specimens are Pleistocene fossils.

Size: 3.8 mm.
Color: White.
Shape: Orbicular; equivalve; subequilateral.
Ornament or sculpture: Compressed; rather smooth except for fine, irregular growth lines.
Hinge area: Umbones low and pointing forward; lunule oval; hinge margin thick but teeth weakly defined.
Pallial line & interior: Pallial line simple with 2 muscle scars; anterior scar elongate.
Habitat: Open bays and inlet-influenced areas; infaunal.
Localities: Entire, more to south.
Occurrence: Common.
Range: Western coast of Florida to Texas.
Remarks: Some writers place in genus *Megaxinus* Brugnone, 1880; [*Lucina floridana*].

Family UNGULINIDAE
  H. & A. Adams, 1857

Genus *Diplodonta* Bronn, 1831
Subgenus *Phlyctiderma* Dall, 1899

Pimpled Diplodon
Diplodonta (Phlyctiderma) semiaspera
  Philippi, 1836

Range: North Carolina to Florida; Texas; Yucatán; West Indies; Brazilian coast to Uruguay.
Remarks: Found by breaking jetty rocks, also in old *Crassostrea* and *Mercenaria* shells; builds nests around itself of mud and sand held together with mucus; does not appear to be equipped to bore.

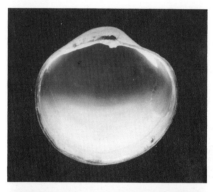

Size: Up to 12 mm.
Color: Chalky white.
Shape: Orbicular, inflated; equivalve.
Ornament or sculpture: Thin shell marked with numerous concentric rows of microscopic pimples.
Hinge area: Two cardinal teeth in each valve; laterals absent; left anterior and right posterior ones split.
Pallial line & interior: Pallial line simple with 2 elongate muscle scars.
Habitat: Open-bay centers, jetties, inlet-influenced areas; infaunal.
Localities: Entire.
Occurrence: Fairly common.

Diplodonta (Phlyctiderma) cf. *D. soror*
  C. B. Adams, 1852

Size: 8–18 mm.
Color: Translucent white.
Shape: Orbicular, inflated.
Ornament or sculpture: Smooth with only fine concentric growth lines; microscopic roughness on slightly compressed posterior slope.
Hinge area: 2 cardinal teeth in each valve, no laterals.
Pallial line & interior: Pallial line simple with 2 muscle scars.
Habitat: Inlet-influenced areas; infaunal.
Localities: Entire, more to south.
Occurrence: Fairly common in beach drift.
Range: Texas to Jamaica; Yucatán.
Remarks: Has been reported as *D. punctata* (Say, 1822).

Order HIPPURITOIDEA Newell, 1965
= [PACHYDONTA Steinman, 1903]
Superfamily CHAMACEA Blainvilie,
1825
Family CHAMIDAE Lamarck, 1809

Genus *Chama* Linné, 1758

Little Corrugated Jewel Box
Chama congregata Conrad, 1833

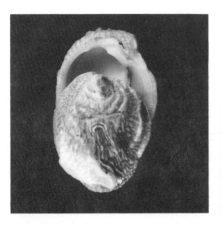

Size: Up to 25 mm.
Color: Red.
Shape: Round; right, or upper, valve much smaller than left.
Ornament or sculpture: Surface covered with numerous low axial corrugations; left valve attached; umbones twist to right; never has foliaceous appearance of *C. macerophylla*.
Hinge area: Umbones turn from right to left; 2 cardinal teeth, 1 heavy and rough in left valve, 2 widely separated small teeth in right; both valves with 1 small posterior lateral tooth.
Pallial line & interior: Pallial line simple, connecting 2 muscle scars.
Habitat: Offshore on calcareous banks; cemented epifaunal.
Occurrence: Uncommon beach shell.
Range: North Carolina to Florida; Texas; West Indies; Central America.
Remarks: Usually only badly eroded right valves found in drift; shell often found attached to valves of *Atrina serrata* (Sowerby, 1815).

Leafy Jewel Box
Chama macerophylla (Gmelin, 1791)
[See *SST*, p. 213]

Genus *Pseudochama* Odhner, 1917

Atlantic Left-Handed Jewel Box
Pseudochama radians (Lamarck, 1819)
[See *SST*, p. 213]

Genus *Arcinella* Schumacher, 1817

True Spiny Jewel Box
Arcinella cornuta Conrad, 1866

Size: 25–38 mm.
Color: White.
Shape: Quadrate, inflated.
Ornament or sculpture: 7 to 9 radial rows of heavy, short spines; heavy shell; coarse granulations between ribs.
Hinge area: Umbones curved forward over large, wide, heart-shaped lunule; large cardinal tooth in left valve.
Pallial line & interior: Pallial line simple, connecting 2 muscle scars.
Habitat: Offshore on calcareous banks; cemented epifaunal.
Localities: Entire, more to south.
Occurrence: Fairly common on beach.
Range: North Carolina; Florida; Texas to Carmen, Campeche, Mexico; Yucatán.
Remarks: Begins and ends life free swimming (attached by right valve in interim); near Port Mansfield jetty; probably Pleistocene fossils; [*Echinochama cornuta*].

Superfamily LEPTONACEA Gray, 1847
Family KELLIIDAE Forbes & Hanley,
1848

Genus *Aligena* H. C. Lea, 1843

Texas Aligena
Aligena texasiana Harry, 1969

Size: 4.8 mm.
Color: Chalky white.
Shape: Subtrigonal, inflated; equivalve;
almost equilateral.
Ornament or sculpture: Smooth, except
for microscopic, concentric growth
lines; both posterior and anterior ends
rounded; ventral margin almost straight
but shows slight depression about
midway; valves very thin.
Hinge area: Beaks rounded, touching;
no escutcheon or lunule; single tooth in
each valve, projecting beyond midline
and larger in right valve.
Pallial line & interior: Two suboval
adductor scars, about equal in size;
pallial line simple but broken into series
of subtriangular marks.

Habitat: Shallow bays; probably
commensal.
Localities: Entire.
Occurrence: Fairly common in beach
drift.
Range: Louisiana; Texas.
Remarks: Holotype collected by
Harold Harry at West Galveston Bay,
Texas, in 1969; probably polychaete
worm associates (burrowing
invertebrates).

Family LEPTONIDAE Gray, 1847

Genus *Lepton* Turton, 1822

Lepton cf. *L. lepidum* Say, 1826

Size: 5 mm.
Color: White, translucent.
Shape: Trigonal; equilateral; equivalve.
Ornament or sculpture: Smooth and
glassy appearing but with numerous
microscopic, longitudinal striations that
curve toward anterior edge on anterior
margin and toward posterior edge on
posterior margin.
Hinge area: Cardinal teeth obsolete;
lateral teeth prominent.
Pallial line & interior: Pallial line
simple.

Habitat: Along shore; epifaunal.
Localities: Entire.
Occurrence: Fairly common in beach drift.
Range: Charleston harbor, South Carolina; Texas.
Remarks: Commensal with other invertebrates; attached to host by byssus.

Family MONTACUTIDAE Clark, 1855

Genus *Mysella* Angas, 1877

Atlantic Flat Lepton
Mysella planulata (Stimpson, 1851)

Size: 3.5 mm.
Color: White.
Shape: Oblong oval, flattened; equivalve; inequilateral.
Ornament or sculpture: Smooth with only fine concentric growth lines.
Hinge area: Small pointed beaks three-fourths of distance back from anterior end; dorsal margin depressed in front and back of beaks.

Pallial line & interior: Pallial line simple with 2 suboval, almost equal muscle scars.
Habitat: Attaches to pilings, buoys, grasses in bays and shallow water; epifaunal.
Localities: Entire.
Occurrence: Fairly common in beach drift.
Range: Greenland to Texas; West Indies.
Remarks: Easily overlooked and confused with *Aligena texasiana*.

Superfamily CARDITACEA Fleming, 1820
Family CARDITIDAE Fleming, 1820
Subfamily CARDITAMERINAE Chavan, 1969

Genus *Carditamera* Conrad, 1838

Broad-Ribbed Cardita
Carditamera floridana Conrad, 1838

Size: 25–63 mm.
Color: Whitish, with small bars of chestnut brown arranged concentrically on ribs.
Shape: Oval; equivalve; inequilateral.
Ornament or sculpture: 15 to 18 strong radiating ribs, beaded by transverse growth lines; beaks close together.
Hinge area: External hinge ligament; hinge oblique; strong cardinal teeth; right valve has 1 anterior lateral, left valve 1 posterior lateral tooth; lunule small, deeply indented under beaks.
Pallial line & interior: Interior smooth with 2 muscle scars.

Habitat: Inlet-influenced areas and hypersaline lagoons; infaunal.
Localities: Southern half of coast.
Occurrence: Common beach shell.
Range: Southern half of Florida; southern Texas to Mexico; Gulf of Campeche; Yucatán; Quintana Roo.
Remarks: Attaches by byssus; dead shells are common, but to date none found alive; probably fossil; [*Cardita floridana*].

Superfamily CRASSATELLACEA Férussac, 1821
Family CRASSATELLIDAE Férussac, 1821
Subfamily SCAMBULINAE Chavan, 1852

Genus *Crassinella* Guppy, 1874

Lunate Crasinella
Crassinella lunulata (Conrad, 1834)

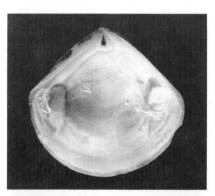

Size: 6–8 mm.
Color: Whitish or pinkish; interior brown; very colorful.
Shape: Trigonal; slightly inequivalve.
Ornament or sculpture: Beaks at middle; valves lapped so posterior dorsal margin of left valve more visible than right; flattened valves sculptured with well-developed concentric ribs and microscopic articulation.
Hinge area: Ligament internal; 2 cardinal teeth on each side, 1 anterior lateral in right, 1 posterior in left.
Pallial line & interior: Pallial line simple, joining 2 adductor muscle scars.
Habitat: Inlet-influenced areas and channels on shelly bottom; infaunal.
Localities: Entire.
Occurrence: Fairly common.
Range: Bermuda; Cape Cod south to Florida; northern Gulf of Mexico; Yucatán; Quintana Roo; West Indies; northern and northeastern Brazil.
Remarks: Syn. *C. quadelupensis* Orbigny, 1846.

Superfamily CARDIACEA Lamarck, 1809
Family CARDIIDAE Lamarck, 1809
Subfamily TRACHYCARDIINAE Stewart, 1930

Genus *Trachycardium* Mörch, 1853
Subgenus *Trachycardium* s.s.

Prickly Cockle
Trachycardium (Trachycardium) isocardia (Linné, 1758)

Size: 76 mm.
Color: Exterior light cream with blotches of red brown; wide band of salmon pink along interior margins.
Shape: Oval, elongated heart-shaped from side.
Ornament or sculpture: 31 to 37 strong, radiating ribs with imbricated scales.
Hinge area: Ligament external, posterior; cardinal teeth arched; umbones prominent, nearly central.
Pallial line & interior: Pallial line simple, connecting 2 white muscle scars; margins crenulate.
Habitat: Offshore; infaunal.
Localities: Central, south.
Occurrence: Uncommon beach shell.
Range: Bermuda; Texas to Mexico; Campeche Bank; Surinam; West Indies to northern coast of South America.
Remarks: Lives offshore and common along Mexican Gulf beaches but only occasional straggler to Texas shore; South Padre most likely location.

sharply scaled ribs; scales on anterior slope on anterior side of ribs, while on central and posterior slopes on posterior side of ribs; separation marked by several ribs with double rows of spines.
Hinge area: Umbones prominent, nearly central; ligament external; cardinal and lateral teeth present.
Pallial line & interior: Interior margin crenate; pallial line indistinct, simple, connecting 2 equal-sized adductor muscle scars.
Habitat: Inlet-influenced areas and bay margins; infaunal.
Localities: Entire.
Occurrence: Fairly common.
Range: North Carolina to Florida; Texas; Carmen, Campeche, Mexico; Gulf of Campeche; Yucatán; West Indies; Surinam; Brazil to Uruguay.
Remarks: After sustained freeze will pop out of sandy mud along lower bay margins; double siphons short and foot well developed for digging.

Subgenus *Dallocardia* Stewart, 1930

Yellow Cockle
Trachycardium (Dallocardia) muricatum (Linné, 1758)

Subfamily LAEVICARDIINAE Keen, 1936

Genus *Laevicardium* Swainson, 1840

Common Egg Cockle
Laevicardium laevigatum (Linné, 1758)

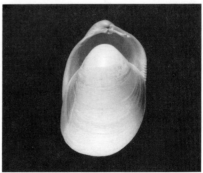

Size: 51 mm.
Color: Light cream with blotches of red brown or shades of yellow; interior white.
Shape: Subcircular, inflated; equivalve.
Ornament or sculpture: 30 to 40

Size: 25 – 51 mm.
Color: Cream colored or pale yellow variably mottled with brown.
Shape: Obliquely egg-shaped.

Ornament or sculpture: Smooth, polished with obscure radiating ribs.
Hinge area: Umbones rounded; cardinal and lateral teeth present.
Pallial line & interior: Interior cream colored with finely serrated margins; pallial line simple, connecting 2 muscle scars; ventral margin crenulate.
Habitat: Offshore; infaunal.
Localities: Central, south.
Occurrence: Uncommon beach shell.
Range: Bermuda; North Carolina to both sides of Florida; Texas; Campeche Bank; Yucatán; Central America; West Indies; Surinam; Brazil.
Remarks: Common on upper Mexican coast and straggler on southern part of Texas coast.

Morton's Egg Cockle
Laevicardium mortoni (Conrad, 1830)

Size: 16–25 mm.
Color: Exterior cream colored, irregularly patterned with brown; interior yellow with brown mottlings.
Shape: Oval, inflated; equivalve.
Ornament or sculpture: Smooth, polished with faint concentric lines microscopically pimpled; shell thin.
Hinge area: Cardinal and lateral teeth present; anterior laterals prominent.
Pallial line & interior: Pallial line simple, connecting 2 muscle scars; margins may or may not be crenulated.
Habitat: Shallow water in inlet-

influenced areas and hypersaline lagoons; infaunal.
Localities: Entire, more common in south.
Occurrence: Common.
Range: Cape Cod to Florida; Texas to Tecolutla, Mexico; Yucatán; Quintana Roo; West Indies.
Remarks: Can swim and hop about in shallow waters with surprising speed. Ducks love it.

Subgenus *Dinocardium* Dall, 1900

Giant Atlantic Cockle
Laevicardium (Dinocardium) robustum (Lightfoot, 1786)

Size: 76–101 mm.
Color: Pale tan, mottled with red brown; posterior slope mahogany brown; interior salmon pink.
Shape: Obliquely ovate, inflated; equivalve.
Ornament or sculpture: 32 to 36 rounded, radial smoothish ribs.
Hinge area: Umbones rounded; heavy external ligament; 1 cardinal tooth in each valve, with 2 anterior lateral and 1 posterior lateral in right valve; complementary arrangement in left valve.
Pallial line & interior: Pallial line simple, connecting 2 muscle scars; margins crenulate.
Habitat: Close to shore and in inlet-influenced areas; infaunal.

Localities: Entire.
Occurrence: Common.
Range: Virginia to northern Florida;
Texas; Carmen, Campeche, Mexico.
Remarks: Largest cockle on Texas
coast; storms often wash great numbers
in alive; juveniles found living in mud
flats in bays around Aransas Pass and
adults at San Luis Pass; [*Dinocardium
robustum*].

Superfamily MACTRACEA Lamarck,
1809
Family MACTRIDAE Lamarck, 1809
Subfamily MACTRINAE Lamarck,
1809

Genus *Mactra* Linné, 1767

Fragile Atlantic Mactra
Mactra fragilis Gmelin, 1791

Size: 38–63 mm.
Color: White.
Shape: Oval; equivalve; subequilateral.
Ornament or sculpture: Margins
rounded; sculpture of fine, irregular
growth lines; posterior slope with 2
radial ridges; fairly large posterior
gape.
Hinge area: Umbones rounded, almost
central; 2 ligaments, 1 external, inner
cartilaginous ligament housed in
spoon-shaped chondrophore posterior
to bifid cardinal tooth.
Pallial line & interior: Polished white
interior with lightly impressed scars of
about equal size and shape; pallial
sinus short, broadly rounded.

Habitat: Open-bay margins; infaunal.
Localities: Entire, more in south.
Occurrence: Fairly common.
Range: North Carolina to Florida;
Texas; West Indies; Surinam.
Remarks: Syn. *M. brasiliana* Lamarck,
1818.

Genus *Mulinia* Gray, 1837

Dwarf Surf Clam
Mulinia lateralis (Say, 1822)

Size: 8–16 mm.
Color: Whitish to cream.
Shape: Trigonal, inflated; inequilateral.
Ornament or sculpture: Smooth except
for fine growth lines; posterior slope
marked with distinct radial ridge.
Hinge area: Umbones high, almost
central; chondrophore, bifid cardinals,
lateral teeth make up hinge complex.
Pallial line & interior: Anterior
adductor scar more elongate than
posterior scar; pallial sinus short,
rounded, oblique.
Habitat: Clayey sediments in every type
of assemblage; infaunal.
Localities: Entire.
Occurrence: Very common.
Range: Maine to northern Florida;
Texas; Gulf of Campeche; Yucatán.
Remarks: Most abundant and ubiqui-
tous bivalve on Texas coast due to abili-
ty to withstand wide range of salinities;
juveniles thin and opalescent, coming to
shore in vast numbers in winter months.

Genus *Rangia* Des Moulins, 1832
Subgenus *Rangia* s.s.

Common Rangia
Rangia (Rangia) cuneata (Gray, 1831)

Subgenus *Rangianella* Conrad, 1868

Brown Rangia
Rangia (Rangianella) flexuosa (Conrad, 1839)

Size: 25–80 mm.
Color: Whitish.
Shape: Obliquely ovate; equivalve; inequilateral.
Ornament or sculpture: Heavy, thick shell sculptured with fine concentric growth lines.
Hinge area: Deeply excavated chondrophore, cardinals, 2 lateral teeth; posterior lateral very long, reaching almost to ventral margin, easily separating it from *R. flexuosa*; umbones prominent, nearer anterior end.
Pallial line & interior: Anterior adductor scar smaller than posterior scar; pallial sinus small but distinct, directed forward and upward.
Habitat: River-influenced areas; infaunal.
Localities: East and central, more prevalent centrally.
Occurrence: Common.
Range: New Jersey; northwestern Florida to Texas and to Alvarado, Veracruz, Mexico.
Remarks: Found a few miles up Nueces River, but is brackish-water species; recent studies indicate that suspended solids in water above substratum where *Rangia* live more significantly inhibit their growth than do characteristics of substratum itself.

Size: 25–60 mm.
Color: Whitish.
Shape: Obliquely ovate, fairly wedge-shaped; inequilateral.
Ornament or sculpture: Thick, heavy shell with sculpture of fine growth lines; long posterior slope keeled.
Hinge area: Umbones prominent; chondrophore present with cardinal teeth, but laterals much shorter than in *R. cuneata*.
Pallial line & interior: 2 rounded adductor muscle scars; pallial sinus almost obsolete.
Habitat: River-influenced areas; infaunal.
Localities: Entire, more to east.
Occurrence: Uncommon.
Range: Louisiana to Texas; Veracruz, Mexico.
Remarks: Can withstand very low salinity, as does *R. cuneata*, but more marine than latter; juvenile specimens easily confused with *Mulinia lateralis*; subgenus *Rangianella* closely related to *Mulinia*; Dall states often can be distinguished only by smaller pallial sinus and inconspicuous "hook" on proximal end of anterior lateral tooth; some have elevated *Rangianella* to generic rank.

Genus *Spisula* Gray, 1837
Subgenus *Hemimactra* Swainson, 1840

Atlantic Surf Clam
Spisula (Hemimactra) solidissima
 similis (Say, 1822)

Subfamily PTEROPSELLINAE Keen,
 1969

Genus *Anatina* Schumacher, 1817

Smooth Duck Clam
Anatina anatina (Spengler, 1802)

Size: 101–127 mm.
Color: Yellowish white.
Shape: Oval.
Ornament or sculpture: Smooth except for fine, concentric growth lines.
Hinge area: Large, shallow, triangular umbones acute, more anteriorly located; chondrophore; 2 cardinal teeth, those in left valve fused at upper ends; opposite deep socket in lateral teeth.
Pallial line & interior: Adductor muscle scars rounded, above middle of valve; pallial sinus short, rounded, almost parallel to pallial line.
Habitat: Inlet-influenced areas; infaunal.
Localities: Entire.
Occurrence: Fairly common beach shell.
Range: Cape Cod; both sides of Florida; Texas.
Remarks: Edible bivalve but not in commercial quantities; syn. *S. s. raveneli* (Conrad, 1831).

Size: 50–76 mm.
Color: White.
Shape: Trigonal; inequilateral.
Ornament or sculpture: Thin, fragile, gaping posteriorly; fairly smooth, except for fine growth lines and concentric ribs near umbones; distinct radial rib on posterior end.
Hinge area: Prominent chondrophore and 3 small cardinal teeth anterior to chondrophore; lateral tooth posterior to chondrophore; umbones high, pointed backward.
Pallial line & interior: Anterior adductor scar elongate; posterior scar rounded; pallial sinus narrow, deep.
Habitat: Surf zone to 40 fathoms; infaunal.
Localities: Entire.
Occurrence: Uncommon beach shell.
Range: North Carolina to northern two-thirds of Florida; Texas; Mexico; Puerto Rico; Brazil.
Remarks: Seldom found except in winter; less common than *Raeta plicatella*; syn. *Labiosa lineata* (Say, 1822).

Genus *Raeta* Gray, 1853

Channeled Duck Clam
Raeta plicatella (Lamarck, 1818)

Family MESODESMATIDAE Gray, 1839
Subfamily ERVILIINAE Dall, 1895

Genus *Ervilia* Turton, 1822

Ervilia cf. *E. concentrica* (Holmes, 1860)

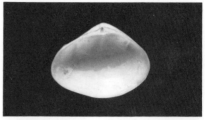

Size: 50–76 mm.
Color: White.
Shape: Trigonal; inequilateral.
Ornament or sculpture: Thin, fragile, gaping posteriorly; sculpture of evenly spaced, rounded concentric ribs with fine striations in intercostal spaces; fine radial threads.
Hinge area: Prominent chondrophore; small, irregular cardinal teeth; single lateral tooth posterior to chondrophore; umbones high, pointed backward.
Pallial line & interior: Anterior adductor scar elongate; posterior scar to about midshell almost parallel to pallial line, somewhat pointed.
Habitat: Probably does not burrow but lives on side on sandy bottom of outer surf zone; epifaunal.
Localities: Entire.
Occurrence: Fairly common.
Range: North Carolina to Florida; Texas; Mexico; West Indies; Surinam; Brazil to Argentina.
Remarks: More common on beaches in winter; syn. *Anatina canaliculata* (Say, 1822).

Size: 5–6 mm.
Color: White.
Shape: Elliptical; equilateral.
Ornament or sculpture: Sculpture of fine, numerous concentric lines; quite variable.
Hinge area: Umbones central; resilium small, internal; cardinal tooth bifid; laterals small.
Pallial line & interior: Muscle scars faintly impressed; pallial sinus rounded, broad, short.
Habitat: Near shore; infaunal.
Localities: Entire, more to south.
Occurrence: Fairly common in beach drift.
Range: Bermuda; North Carolina to both sides of Florida; Texas; Quintana Roo; West Indies to Brazil.
Remarks: Because of similarity to juvenile *Mulinias*, may have been long overlooked on Texas coast.

Superfamily SOLENACEA Lamarck, 1809
Family SOLENIDAE Lamarck, 1809

Genus *Solen* Linné, 1758

Green Jackknife Clam
Solen viridis Say, 1822

Family CULTELLIDAE Davis, 1935

Genus *Ensis* Schumacher, 1817

Jackknife Clam
Ensis minor Dall, 1900

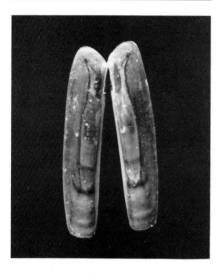

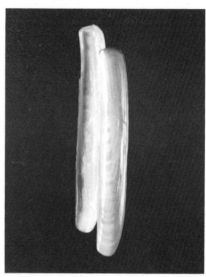

Size: Up to 51 mm.
Color: White.
Shape: Long, narrow, flattened cylindrical; equivalve.
Ornament or sculpture: Dorsal edge straight; ventral edge curved; fragile.
Hinge area: Single projecting tooth at very end of valve.
Pallial line & interior: Pallial line has 2 muscle scars and pallial sinus.
Habitat: Inlets, near shore; infaunal.
Localities: East.
Occurrence: Uncommon.
Range: Rhode Island to northern Florida; Gulf states.
Remarks: Western Louisiana species easily confused with *Ensis minor* but much shorter; figure that of juvenile.

Size: Up to 76 mm.
Color: Shell white; interior purplish.
Shape: Cylindrical; equivalve.
Ornament or sculpture: Long narrow shell smooth, fragile.
Hinge area: Left valve has 2 vertical cardinal teeth; each valve has long low posterior tooth; teeth in less pointed end.
Pallial line & interior: 2 adductor muscle scars; pallial sinus shallow.
Habitat: Enclosed lagoon and bay margins; infaunal.
Localities: Entire.
Occurrence: Common.
Range: New Jersey to Florida to Texas.
Remarks: A favorite food of wading birds.

Superfamily TELLINACEA Blainville, 1824
Family TELLINIDAE Blainville, 1824
Subfamily TELLININAE Blainville, 1824

Genus *Tellina* Linné, 1758
Subgenus *Angulus* Megerle von Mühlfeld, 1811

Tampa Tellin
Tellina (Angulus) tampaensis Conrad, 1866

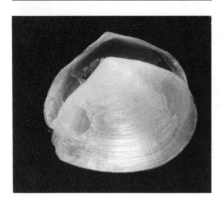

Size: 13–24 mm.
Color: Smooth white, frequently suffused with pale peach coloration; interior polished.
Shape: Ovate subtrigonal; inequivalve; inequilateral.
Ornament or sculpture: Anterior margin broadly rounded; posterior dorsal margin steeply sloping; sculpture of concentric lines separated by narrow, well-defined sulci.
Hinge area: Ligament brown, external; cardinal teeth present, but no true lateral teeth produced.
Pallial line & interior: Adductor muscle scars well impressed; anterior scar longer, narrower, higher than posterior scar; pallial sinus descends to pallial line in short, straight drop some distance from anterior scar.
Habitat: Hypersaline lagoons; infaunal.
Localities: Entire.
Occurrence: Fairly common.

Range: Southern half of Florida to Texas; Bahamas; Cuba.
Remarks: Look along Packery Channel.

Say's Tellin
Tellina (Angulus) texana Dall, 1900

Size: 16.5 mm.
Color: White with opalescent interior.
Shape: Subelliptical to subtrigonal; inequivalve; inequilateral.
Ornament or sculpture: Anterior margin rounded; posterior dorsal margin elongate, steeply inclined; sculpture of weak, finely incised, closely spaced concentric sulci.
Hinge area: Ligament yellowish brown, strong, external; cardinal teeth but no true lateral teeth; umbones posterior to middle, blunt.
Pallial line & interior: Adductor muscle scars fairly well impressed; anterior scar elongate, rounded below; posterior scar rounded; pallial sinus convex above, gently inclined and slightly concave anteriorly, falling in arch to pallial line near but not touching anterior scar.
Habitat: Bay centers; infaunal.
Localities: East, central.
Occurrence: Fairly common.
Range: North Carolina to southern half of Florida; Texas; Cuba.
Remarks: Holotype collected by J. A. Singley at Corpus Christi Bay, Texas, ca. 1893; tolerates lower salinity than other Texas tellins; syn. *T. sayi* Dall, 1900.

DeKay's Dwarf Tellin
Tellina (Angulus) versicolor DeKay, 1843

Subgenus *Eurytellina* Fischer, 1887

Alternate Tellin
Tellina (Eurytellina) alternata Say, 1822

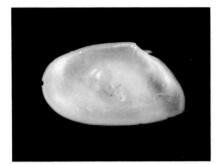

Size: 14 mm.
Color: Translucent with red, white, or pink rays; shiny.
Shape: Elongate, subelliptical.
Ornament or sculpture: Anterior dorsal margin elongate, slightly inclined; posterior dorsal margin steeply inclined, short, slightly concave; posterior marked with rounded keel; sculpture of widely spaced, strongly incised concentric sulci; no radial sculpture.
Hinge area: Umbones just posterior to middle, depressed, pointed; ligament yellowish brown, external; right valve has cardinal teeth and weak laterals; left valve has cardinal teeth but no laterals.
Pallial line & interior: Anterior adductor scar elongate, rounded below; posterior scar rounded; pallial sinus rises gently posteriorly, convex above, arches down to pallial line very near anterior scar, at times touching it.
Habitat: Bays and offshore in sandy mud; infaunal.
Localities: Entire.
Occurrence: Common.
Range: Rhode Island to southern half of Florida; Texas; Campeche Bank; West Indies.
Remarks: Without magnification can be confused with *T. iris* but lacks distinctive oblique sculpture of *T. iris*.

Size: 70 mm.
Color: Glossy white, often with slight blushes of pink or yellow.
Shape: Elongate, subtrigonal; inequivalve; inequilateral.
Ornament or sculpture: Outline narrow posteriorly with slight truncation; sculpture of incised concentric lines separated by broad bands; left valve has broader bands and fewer lines than right; posterior ridge occurs in right valve; every alternate striation disappears at angle of keel.
Hinge area: Umbones slightly posterior to center, small, scarcely elevated; ligament strong, brown, exterior; 3 cardinal teeth in right valve; both valves have internal rib extending from umbo to anterior muscle scar.
Pallial line & interior: Adductor muscle scars well impressed; pallial sinus curves upward toward umbones, extends anteriorly almost to muscle scar.
Habitat: Sand near shore, bay margins, inlets; infaunal.
Localities: Entire, more to east.
Occurrence: Fairly common.
Range: North Carolina; Florida; Gulf states; Yucatán; Costa Rica; West Indies; southern Brazil.
Remarks: Until recently considered closely related to *T. a. tayloriana*; valves of *T. alternata* somewhat more inflated and range much wider.

Taylor's Tellin
Tellina (Eurytellina) alternata
tayloriana Sowerby, 1867

Rose Petal Tellin
Tellina (Eurytellina) lineata Turton,
1819

Size: 63 mm.
Color: Glossy pink.
Shape: Elongate subtrigonal;
inequivalve; inequilateral.
Ornament or sculpture: Outline
narrows posteriorly and truncated at
end; sculpture of incised concentric
lines, separated by broad bands;
sculpture stronger and closer on right
valve.
Hinge area: Ligament brown, external;
3 cardinal teeth and 2 laterals in right
valve; heavy rib extends from umbones
to anterior adductor scar in both
valves.
Pallial line & interior: Pallial sinus
variable but usually about equal in each
valve, flattened across top and
extending almost to anterior scar,
where it drops rather abruptly to pallial
line.
Habitat: Near shore, 3.6 to 21.6 meters
(2 to 12 fathoms); inlet areas; infaunal.
Localities: Entire.
Occurrence: Common.
Range: Gulf coast of Texas and
Mexico.
Remarks: Pink color main distinction
between subspecies and *T. alternata*;
right valve of *T. a. tayloriana*
supposedly much flatter than that of
T. alternata; they may be same species.

Size: 25–34 mm.
Color: Pink to white.
Shape: Elongate subtrigonal; equivalve;
inequilateral.
Ornament or sculpture: Anterior
margin well rounded; posterior dorsal
margin steeply sloping; sculpture of
close, weak, concentric sulci separated
by low, narrow bands; posterior ridge
present but not well developed,
stronger on left valve; twist to right at
posterior end.
Hinge area: Ligament dark brown,
short, wide, sunken; umbones slightly
raised, pointed, inflated, located just
posterior to middle; both cardinal and
lateral teeth present, posterior lateral
well developed; variable anterior rib
between umbones and anterior scar.
Pallial line & interior: Adductor muscle
scars well impressed; pallial sinus
convex above, not rising above
adductor muscle scars, extending closer
to anterior scar than that of
T. alternata tayloriana.
Habitat: Offshore or dead in spoil
banks; infaunal.
Localities: Central.
Occurrence: Uncommon.
Range: All of Florida; Texas; Yucatán;
Costa Rica; West Indies; Brazil.
Remarks: Shape and color variable,
but strong twist of valves to right
posteriorly and umbones pointing to
back are consistent; specimens found
on Texas coast appear to be Pleistocene
fossils; not reported living to date.

Subgenus *Merisca* Dall, 1900

Lintea Tellin
Tellina (Merisca) aequistriata (Say, 1824)

Subgenus *Scissula* Dall, 1900

Iris Tellin
Tellina (Scissula) iris Say, 1822

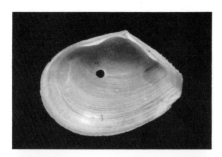

Size: 9–24 mm.
Color: White.
Shape: Moderately oval; inequilateral.
Ornament or sculpture: Sculpture of numerous sharp, concentric ridges; left valve has 1 posterior radial ridge, right valve 2; posterior margin narrow, flexed.
Hinge area: Umbones small, sharp; ligament small; weak hinge area has 2 long laterals in left valve.
Pallial line & interior: Muscle scars small; dorsal line of pallial sinus meets pallial line near anterior scar.
Habitat: Offshore in sand, 5 to 15 meters (9 to 28 fathoms); infaunal.
Localities: Entire.
Occurrence: Fairly common.
Range: North Carolina to Florida; Texas; Campeche Bank; Yucatán; West Indies; Brazilian coast to Bahia.
Remarks: Syn. *Quadrans lintea* Conrad, 1837; distinguished by posterior twist.

Size: 15.3 mm.
Color: Transparent to translucent suffused with pink; 2 white rays often occur in posterior quarter.
Shape: Elongate, elliptical; equivalve; inequilateral.
Ornament or sculpture: Anterior dorsal margin long, gently sloping to rounded anterior margin; posterior margin obliquely truncated; posterior slope slightly keeled; sculpture of faint growth lines more developed posteriorly, crossed by well-developed, widely spaced oblique lines.
Hinge area: Umbones posterior to middle, small, slightly pointed; ligament light yellow brown, weak, external; left valve has cardinal teeth but no true lateral teeth; right valve has cardinal teeth and interior lateral tooth but no posterior lateral.
Pallial line & interior: Adductor scars weak; anterior scar irregularly quadrate; posterior scar rounded; pallial sinus rises abruptly posteriorly,

descends gently, arches to pallial line, well separated from anterior scar.
Habitat: Near shore and inlet areas; infaunal.
Localities: Entire.
Occurrence: Common.
Range: Bermuda; North Carolina to Florida; Gulf of Mexico.
Remarks: One of most common in winter drift on Texas beaches.

Genus *Tellidora* H. & A. Adams, 1856

White Crested Tellin
Tellidora cristata (Récluz, 1842)

Size: Up to 37 mm.
Color: White.
Shape: Subtrigonal, very compressed; inequivalve; inequilateral.
Ornament or sculpture: Anterior and posterior dorsal margins have triangular spines; sculpture of strong, narrow, concentric ridges; spines form deep lunule and escutcheon.
Hinge area: Umbones central, acute, elevated; ligament brown, short, partially internal; 2 cardinal teeth in each valve and strong, triangular, anterior lateral tooth in right valve.
Pallial line & interior: Adductor scars well impressed; anterior scar more elongate than posterior; pallial sinus short, widely separated from anterior scar, arches down to pallial line near posterior end.
Habitat: Inlets and channels; bay margins in sandy bottoms; infaunal.

Localities: Entire.
Occurrence: Uncommon.
Range: North Carolina to western Florida and Texas; Yucatán.
Remarks: Dorsal spines make this clam unique.

Genus *Strigilla* Turton, 1822
Subgenus *Pisostrigilla* Olsson, 1961

White Strigilla
Strigilla (Pisostrigilla) mirabilis (Philippi, 1841)

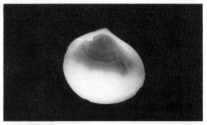

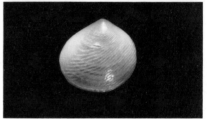

Size: 8 mm.
Color: White, translucent, shiny.
Shape: Oval, inflated; inequivalve; equilateral.
Ornament or sculpture: Sculpture of fine growth lines crossed by oblique lines that meet ventral margin at about 45°; posterior slope patterned with 4 or more zigzag rows of lines.
Hinge area: Umbones rounded, almost central; 2 cardinals and 2 lateral teeth present; left posterior cardinal very thin, fragile.
Pallial line & interior: Large pallial sinus runs forward but does not touch anterior muscle scar; weak cruciform muscle scars near ventral margin.
Habitat: Offshore; infaunal.

Localities: Entire.
Occurrence: Uncommon in beach drift.
Range: Bermuda; southeastern United States; Texas; Campeche Bank; West Indies; northeastern Brazil.
Remarks: Oblique sculpture distinctive among minute Texas bivalves.

Subfamily MACOMINAE Olsson, 1961

Genus *Macoma* Leach, 1819

Tenta Macoma
Macoma tenta (Say, 1834)

Size: 12–25 mm.
Color: White, slightly iridescent.
Shape: Elongate, oblong; inequilateral.
Ornament or sculpture: Smooth except for microscopic growth lines; thin; posterior margin truncated and flexed to right, marked with radial ridge.
Hinge area: Umbones small, sharp; ligament small, brown; 2 cardinal teeth in left valve and 1 in right; 1 posterior lateral tooth.
Pallial line & interior: Anterior adductor scar elongate, posterior rounded; pallial sinus nearly half confluent, almost reaching anterior scar.
Habitat: Open-bay margins; shallow hypersaline lagoons; infaunal.
Localities: Entire.
Occurrence: Common.

Range: Bermuda; Cape Cod to Florida; Texas; Campeche Bank; West Indies; Brazil.
Remarks: Lives in muddy bottoms.

Subgenus *Psammacoma* Dall, 1900

Short Macoma
Macoma (Psammacoma) brevifrons (Say, 1834)

Size: 25 mm.
Color: White to pale peach.
Shape: Oval; inequilateral.
Ornament or sculpture: Shell smooth except for fine growth lines; very weak radial ridge posteriorly.
Hinge area: Umbones small, pointed, anterior to middle; ligament brown, small, external; 2 cardinal teeth in each valve; posterior tooth in left much smaller than others; no lateral teeth.
Pallial line & interior: Scars and pallial line hardly visible; elongate anterior scar and small round posterior scar; pallial sinus large, rounded, almost confluent with pallial line.
Habitat: Near shore, possibly in bays; infaunal.
Localities: Entire.
Occurrence: Fairly common.
Range: North Carolina to Texas; Yucatán; Brazil.
Remarks: Much the same color and size as *Tellina tampaensis*, but shape and hinge area differ; until monograph on macomas is published, *M. brevifrons* and *M. aurora* will be considered synonymous on the basis of published descriptions.

Pulley's Macoma
Macoma (Psammacoma) pulleyi Boyer, 1969

Range: Mississippi delta to eastern Texas[?].
Remarks: Confused with *M. tageliformis,* which is more inequivalve; ligament area depressed and does not have posterior ridge and abrupt ventral angle of *M. pulleyi.*

Tagelus-Like Macoma
Macoma (Psammacoma) tageliformis Dall, 1900

Size: 42–55 mm.
Color: White.
Shape: Elongate, moderately inflated; equivalve; inequilateral.
Ornament or sculpture: Thin; anterior end longer; anterior dorsal margin almost rectilinear; anterior margin rounded above and more gently and evenly curved below; ventral margin nearly straight, subparallel to anterior dorsal margin, intersecting posterior margin abruptly; posterior dorsal margin sloping steeply and meeting posterior margin in curve; smooth except for very fine growth lines; rounded ridge running from umbo to posterior ventral angle marks intersection of posterior slope with surface of disc, stronger in left valve.
Hinge area: Hinge plate narrow; left valve with 1 bifid anterior cardinal and 1 lamellar posterior cardinal; right valve with 1 bifid anterior cardinal and 1 smaller, grooved posterior cardinal.
Pallial line & interior: Pallial sinus rises obliquely, sinuous above, narrowing and extending forward about three-quarters of distance between adductor muscle scars, about half confluent with pallial line below; slight posterior gape.
Habitat: Offshore, mud substratum in delta-influenced water; infaunal.
Localities: East.
Occurrence: Uncommon.

Size: Up to 63 mm.
Color: Dull white.
Shape: Oblong; inequilateral.
Ornament or sculpture: Sculpture of fine, irregular growth lines; posterior slightly flexed to right; heavier than other macomas.
Hinge area: Umbones toward posterior, pointed; ligament external, dark brown; cardinal teeth fairly strong, 2 in each valve; posterior tooth in left valve thin, often obsolete; no laterals.
Pallial line & interior: Anterior adductor scar elongate; posterior scar rounded; large, convex, rounded pallial sinus one-fourth confluent with pallial line.
Habitat: Near shore, 3.6 to 19.8 meters (2 to 11 fathoms) in silty clay; infaunal, probably deep.
Localities: Entire.
Occurrence: Fairly common beach shell.
Range: Louisiana; Texas to Tuxpan, Veracruz, Mexico; Yucatán; West Indies; Surinam; Brazilian coast to São Paulo.

Remarks: Longer and larger than most macomas; holotype collected from Corpus Christi Bay, Texas, by J. A. Singley ca. 1893.

Subgenus *Austromacoma* Leach, 1961

Constricted Macoma
Macoma (Austromacoma) constricta (Bruguière, 1792)

Size: 25–63 mm.
Color: White.
Shape: Subquadrate; inequivalve; inequilateral.
Ornament or sculpture: Sculptured with irregular, fine, concentric growth lines; low radial ridge marks posterior slope, which is flexed to right.
Hinge area: Umbones rounded; ligament long, narrow; cardinal teeth weak; no laterals.
Pallial line & interior: Muscle scars and pallial line weak; 2 rather high muscle scars; pallial sinus extended to near anterior scar, convex above and correspondingly curved below.
Habitat: Open-bay margins and centers; infaunal.
Localities: Entire.
Occurrence: Fairly common.
Range: Florida to Texas; Yucatán; West Indies; Surinam; Brazil.
Remarks: More tolerant of extremes in salinities and temperatures than other macomas on Texas coast; hole in figured specimen drilled by predatory gastropod; figured specimen more typical of those found in Texas than that shown in *SST*, p. 233.

Subgenus *Rexitherus* Tryon, 1869

Mitchell's Macoma
Macoma (Rexitherus) mitchelli Dall, 1895

Size: 25 mm.
Color: White.
Shape: Elongate, subquadrate; inequilateral.
Ornament or sculpture: Smooth except for faint concentric growth lines; weak radial ridge marks posterior slope.
Hinge area: Umbones low, pointed, more toward posterior; cardinal teeth very weak; no laterals.
Pallial line & interior: Posterior muscle scar larger and more rounded than anterior; pallial sinus large, dorsally convex, gently sloping to pallial line before reaching anterior scar.
Habitat: River-influenced areas, estuaries; infaunal.
Localities: Central and east.
Occurrence: Common.
Range: South Carolina to central Texas.
Remarks: Near rivers in brackish water; holotype collected from Matagorda Bay, Texas, by J. D. Mitchell ca. 1894.

Family DONACIDAE Fleming, 1828

Genus *Donax* Linné, 1758

Fat Little Donax
Donax texasianus Philippi, 1847

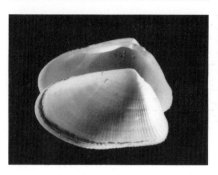

Coquina Shell
Donax roemeri roemeri Philippi, 1847

Size: 8–12 mm.
Color: Whitish with pale blue, pink, or yellow blushes; seldom rayed as is *D. roemeri roemeri*.
Shape: Unequally trigonal; inflated.
Ornament or sculpture: Glossy with fine concentric growth lines; radial threads on blunt posterior end heavily beaded.
Hinge area: Left valve overlaps right on ventral margin; ligament external; 2 cardinal teeth.
Pallial line & interior: Interior smooth; pallial sinus large, rounded.
Habitat: Surf-zone sand; subtidal; infaunal.
Localities: Entire sandy portion.
Occurrence: Fairly common.
Range: Northern shores of Gulf of Mexico; Mexico.
Remarks: Stays in deeper water; holotype collected by F. Roemer at Galveston, Texas, ca. 1846; syn. *D. tumidus* Philippi, 1848.

Size: 12–18 mm.
Color: Variable: often rayed, pink, purple, yellow, white, bluish, or mauve.
Shape: Unequally trigonal or wedge-shaped; equivalve.
Ornament or sculpture: Glossy with fine concentric growth lines and radial striae that become stronger on blunt posterior end.
Hinge area: Umbones low; external ligament behind umbones; cardinal and lateral teeth present.
Pallial line & interior: 2 small muscle scars; large, rounded pallial sinus adjoining posterior scar, extending to middle of shell; margins finely crenate.
Habitat: Surf zone, intertidally year-around; infaunal.
Localities: Entire sandy portion.
Occurrence: Common.
Range: Texas to Alvarado, Veracruz, Mexico.
Remarks: Used to make coquina chowder; has life span of 2 years; feeds on minute organisms on sand grains; dies off in fall; holotype collected by F. Roemer at Galveston, Texas, ca. 1846.

Family PSAMMOBIIDAE Fleming, 1828
Subfamily SANGUINOLARIINAE Grant & Gale, 1931

Genus *Sanguinolaria* Lamarck, 1799

Atlantic Sanguin
Sanguinolaria sanguinolenta (Gmelin, 1791)

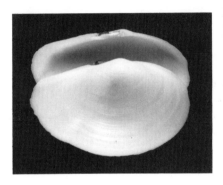

Size: 38–50 mm.
Color: White; umbones and area just below bright orangish red fading into white ventrally.
Shape: Subovate; inequivalve; inequilateral.
Ornament or sculpture: Thin, gaping shell sculptured with microscopic growth lines; left valve slightly more compressed than right.
Hinge area: Hinge teeth near center of dorsal margin; 2 small cardinals in each valve; ligament external.
Pallial line & interior: Large pallial sinus with U-shaped hump at top.
Habitat: Offshore; infaunal.
Localities: Central, south.
Occurrence: Uncommon.
Range: Southern Florida; Gulf states; West Indies; Surinam; almost all of Brazil.
Remarks: Color fades quickly; probably adventitious; wrongly referred to as *S. cruenta* (Lightfoot, 1786).

Family SEMELIDAE Stoliczka, 1870

Genus *Semele* Schumacher, 1817

Cancellate Semele
Semele bellastriata (Conrad, 1837)

Size: 12–18 mm.
Color: Yellowish white with reddish flecks or all purplish gray; interior white suffused with mauve or purple.
Shape: Oval.
Ornament or sculpture: Surface sculptured with concentric ridges and radial riblets stronger on anterior and posterior slopes, giving cancellate appearance at these extremities.
Hinge area: Umbones slightly pointed, just behind center; horizontal chondrophore and 2 cardinal teeth in each valve; right valve has 2 lateral teeth.
Pallial line & interior: 2 rounded muscle scars; pallial sinus deep, rounded.
Habitat: Offshore; infaunal.
Localities: Entire.
Occurrence: Uncommon beach shell.
Range: Bermuda; North Carolina to southern half of Florida; Texas; Campeche Bank; Yucatán; West Indies; Surinam; northeastern Brazil.
Remarks: Found after severe northers near jetties at Port Aransas.

White Atlantic Semele
Semele proficua (Pulteney, 1799)

Purplish Semele
Semele purpurascens (Gmelin, 1791)

Size: 12–35 mm.
Color: Whitish to yellowish white; interior yellowish, glossy, sometimes flecked with mauve.
Shape: Orbicular; equivalve.
Ornament or sculpture: Sculpture of fine, irregular growth lines and microscopic radial lines.
Hinge area: Umbones almost central, pointed; hinge area has long chondrophore to house resilium, 2 small, fragile cardinal teeth; right valve has 2 lateral teeth.
Pallial line & interior: Muscle scars rounded; pallial sinus deep, rounded, oblique.
Habitat: Open-bay centers, inlet areas, near shore; infaunal.
Localities: Entire.
Occurrence: Fairly common.
Range: Bermuda; North Carolina to southern half of Florida; Texas; Yucatán; Central America; West Indies; Brazilian coast to Argentina.
Remarks: Most common *Semele* on Texas coast.

Size: 25–38 mm.
Color: Variable: cream with purplish or orange flecks.
Shape: Oval; equivalve.
Ornament or sculpture: Thin shell sculptured with concentric striae weaker toward posterior margin; microscopic lines between striae but no radial ribs; lines tend to converge.
Hinge area: Umbones posterior of center, pointed; hinge with horizontal chondrophore, 2 cardinal teeth; right valve has 2 lateral teeth.
Pallial line & interior: Muscle scars irregularly shaped; pallial sinus deep, rounded.
Habitat: Offshore on sand bottoms and banks; infaunal.
Localities: Entire, more to south.
Occurrence: Uncommon beach shell.
Range: North Carolina to southern half of Florida; Texas; southern Mexico; Central America; West Indies; Brazilian coast to Uruguay.
Remarks: Only worn shells found.

Genus *Abra* Lamarck, 1818
Subgenus *Abra* s.s.

Common Atlantic Abra
Abra (Abra) aequalis (Say, 1822)

Size: 6 mm.
Color: White.
Shape: Orbicular.
Ornament or sculpture: Smooth, polished; anterior margin of right valve grooved.
Hinge area: Umbones small, pointed; 2 small cardinal teeth in right valve, 1 weak; lateral teeth absent in left valve, 1 anterior lateral in right valve; elongate chondrophore extending posteriorly from cardinal teeth.
Pallial line & interior: Pallial sinus large, directed forward and upward.
Habitat: Open bays, inlet-influenced areas, along shore; infaunal.
Localities: Entire.
Occurrence: Common.
Range: Delaware to Florida; Texas; Gulf of Campeche; Yucatán; West Indies; Surinam; northeastern and eastern Brazil.
Remarks: Next to *Mulinia*, most common bivalve on Texas beaches.

Genus *Cumingia* G. B. Sowerby I, 1833

Tellin-Like Cumingia
Cumingia tellinoides (Conrad, 1831)

Size: 12–18 mm.
Color: White.
Shape: Trigonal.
Ornament or sculpture: Thin shell sculptured with fine, slightly raised growth lines; posterior end slightly pointed, flexed; radial ridge on posterior slope.
Hinge area: Umbones pointed, just posterior to center; both valves have 1 small, bladelike cardinal tooth, 1 central spoon-shaped chondrophore, elongated anterior and posterior laterals.
Pallial line & interior: Anterior adductor scar elongated, posterior scar rounded; latter largely confluent with pallial line below; pallial sinus deep, rounded.
Habitat: Bay margins, high-salinity bays, inlet areas; infaunal.
Localities: Entire.
Occurrence: Fairly common.
Range: Nova Scotia to St. Augustine, Florida; Texas; Cuba.
Remarks: Dead specimens found in holes in rock and oyster shell but more apt to be found in mud among roots.

Family SOLECURTIDAE Orbigny,
1846
Subfamily SOLECURTINAE Orbigny,
1846

Genus *Solecurtus* Blainville, 1824

Corrugated Razor Clam
Solecurtus cumingianus Dunker, 1861

Size: 25–63 mm.
Color: White, dull.
Shape: Elongate cylindrical, flattened;
equivalve.
Ornament or sculpture: Surface of shell
sculptured with irregular growth lines
crossed by fine, oblique lines; both
rounded ends gape.
Hinge area: External ligament posterior
to umbones; right valve has 2 strong
cardinal teeth, left valve 1 cardinal
tooth.
Pallial line & interior: Pallial sinus
extends forward to point below
cardinal teeth.
Habitat: Offshore; infaunal.
Localities: Entire.
Occurrence: Uncommon beach shell.
Range: Southeastern United States;
Texas; Mexico; Campeche Bank; West
Indies; Colombia; Brazil.
Remarks: Single valves on beach of
mid–Padre Island; probably fossil.

Genus *Tagelus* Gray, 1847
Subgenus *Mesopleura* Conrad, 1867

Purplish Tagelus
Tagelus (Mesopleura) divisus (Spengler,
1794)

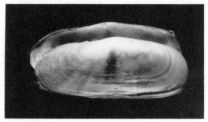

Size: 25–38 mm.
Color: Whitish purple with strong
purple radial streak about midshell.
Shape: Flattened cylindrical, elongate;
equivalve.
Ornament or sculpture: Thin, fragile
shell unsculptured, gaping at both ends.
Hinge area: Umbones posterior of
center, suppressed; cardinal but no
lateral teeth in each valve; purple ray
marks position of weak, internal radial
rib just anterior to teeth.
Pallial line & interior: 2 muscle scars;
pallial sinus deep but does not extend
to cardinal teeth.
Habitat: Open sounds, open-lagoon
margins; infaunal.
Localities: Entire.
Occurrence: Common.
Range: Bermuda; Cape Cod to
southern Florida; Gulf states; Yucatán;
Quintana Roo; Caribbean to Brazil;
Surinam.
Remarks: A favored food of herons.

Stout Tagelus
Tagelus (Mesopleura) plebeius
  (Lightfoot, 1786)

Superfamily DREISSENACEA Gray,
  1840
Family DREISSENIDAE Gray, 1840

Genus *Mytilopsis* Conrad, 1858

Conrad's False Mussel
Mytilopsis leucophaeta (Conrad, 1831)

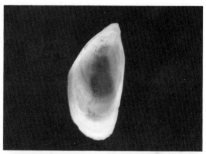

Size: 50–68 mm.
Color: White.
Shape: Elongate, rectangular;
equivalve.
Ornament or sculpture: Strong shell
sculptured with faint, irregular growth
lines; gapes at each end; weak radial
ridge on posterior slope.
Hinge area: Umbones posterior of
center, suppressed; cardinal but no
lateral teeth in each valve; lacks
internal ribs of *T. divisus.*
Pallial line & interior: 2 muscle scars;
pallial sinus deep.
Habitat: Enclosed lagoons, bay
margins; infaunal.
Localities: Entire.
Occurrence: Common.
Range: Cape Cod to southern Florida;
Gulf states; West Indies; Surinam;
Brazilian coast to Bahia Blanca,
Argentina.
Remarks: Buried in mud among roots;
tolerates lower salinities than
T. divisus; syn. *T. gibbus* Spengler,
1794.

Size: 18 mm.
Color: Bluish brown to tan.
Shape: Mussellike.
Ornament or sculpture: Exterior very
rough; anterior end much depressed;
byssal opening small; shelf, or septum,
at beak end.
Hinge area: Long thin bar under
ligament.
Pallial line & interior: Pallial line
simple with 2 adductor muscle scars.
Habitat: Brackish water; epifaunal.
Localities: Entire.
Occurrence: Fairly common.
Range: New York to Florida to Texas
and Mexico.
Remarks: Internal septum across end
distinguishes it from mussel; attaches in
clusters by byssal thread; [*Congeria
leucophaeta*].

Superfamily CORBICULACEA Gray, 1847
Family CORBICULIDAE Gray, 1847

Genus *Polymesoda* Rafinesque, 1820

Carolina Marsh Clam
Polymesoda caroliniana (Bosc, 1802)

Subgenus *Pseudocyrena* Bourguignat, 1854

Florida Marsh Clam
Polymesoda (Pseudocyrena) maritima
(Orbigny, 1842)

Size: 25 mm.
Color: Whitish flushed with purple pink; interior white with wide purple margin or all purple.
Shape: Trigonal; equivalve; inequilateral.
Ornament or sculpture: Smooth with weak, irregular growth lines; not heavy; ventral margin slightly sinuate posteriorly.
Hinge area: Each hinge with 3 small almost vertical teeth below umbones and each hinge with 1 anterior and posterior lateral.
Pallial line & interior: Pallial sinus narrow, ascending, fairly deep with 2 adductor muscle scars.
Habitat: In sand in open hypersaline bays and inlets; infaunal.
Localities: Central, south.
Occurrence: Common.
Range: Key West to northern Florida; Texas; Yucatán; Quintana Roo.
Remarks: Seldom found in Galveston area; syn. *Pseudocyrena floridana* (Conrad, 1846).

Size: 25–38 mm.
Color: White.
Shape: Trigonal, inflated; equivalve; inequilateral.
Ornament or sculpture: Rather smooth with weak concentric growth lines.
Hinge area: Erosion of umbones typical; umbones elevated; each hinge with 3 small, almost vertical, equally sized teeth below umbones and each hinge with 1 anterior and posterior lateral; dark brown, long, narrow ligament external.
Pallial line & interior: Pallial sinus narrow, ascending, fairly deep with 2 equal adductor muscle scars.
Habitat: Estuaries; infaunal.
Localities: All but southern tip of coast, more in Matagorda Bay and east.
Occurrence: Fairly common.
Range: Virginia to northern half of Florida and Texas.
Remarks: Can stand very brackish to fresh water; common in middle part of Texas coast; found alive in Lavaca Bay; rare on other parts of coast.

Superfamily VENERACEA Rafinesque, 1815
Family VENERIDAE Rafinesque, 1815
Subfamily PITARINAE Stewart, 1930

Genus *Callocardia* A. Adams, 1864
Subgenus *Agriopoma* Dall, 1902

Texas Venus
Callocardia (Agriopoma) texasiana
(Dall, 1892)

Range: Northwestern Florida to Texas and Mexico.
Remarks: May be assigned to genus *Pitar*; lives just below sand; live specimens rare on Texas shores but worn valves fairly common in Galveston area and less so on rest of coast; holotype collected by Wuerdemann ca. 1856 from Galveston, Texas.

Genus *Callista* Poli, 1791
Subgenus *Macrocallista* Meek, 1876

Calico Clam
Callista (Macrocallista) maculata
(Linné, 1758) [See *SST*, p. 241]

Sunray Venus
Callista (Macrocallista) nimbosa
(Lightfoot, 1786)

Size: 38–76 mm.
Color: Creamy white to dirty gray; interior chalky white.
Shape: Oval elongate, inflated; equivalve; inequilateral.
Ornament or sculpture: Smooth with only very fine concentric growth lines.
Hinge area: Umbones prominent, rolled in under themselves; weak, tear-shaped lunule; 3 cardinal teeth; posterior cardinal S-shaped in right valve; left anterior lateral small and fitting into socket in right valve.
Pallial line & interior: 2 small muscle scars, anterior scar very close to margin; pallial line strong with deep, triangular sinus touching posterior scar; margin smooth.
Habitat: Clay lagoon centers and along shore in clay; infaunal.
Localities: Entire.
Occurrence: Fairly common beach shell.

Size: 101–127 mm.
Color: Pale salmon with broken, brownish radial lines.
Shape: Elongated oval; equivalve; inequilateral.
Ornament or sculpture: Polished; sculpture of inconspicuous radial and concentric lines.
Hinge area: Umbones depressed; lunule impressed, oval, purplish; long external ligament; 3 cardinal teeth.
Pallial line & interior: 2 muscle scars; pallial sinus reflected, wider at base, angled at end; margins smooth.
Habitat: Shallow sandy bottoms, inlet-influenced areas; infaunal.

Localities: Entire, more to south.
Occurrence: Uncommon beach shell.
Range: North Carolina to Florida and Gulf states.
Remarks: Abundant in past, because tools and scrapers made from it found in Indian middens along bays; occurs buried in sand when living, but Texas specimens probably fossil.

Subfamily DOSINIINAE Deshayes, 1853

Genus *Dosinia* Scopoli, 1777

Disk Dosinia
Dosinia discus (Reeve, 1850)

Size: 50–76 mm.
Color: White.
Shape: Lenticular, flattened; equivalve; inequilateral.
Ornament or sculpture: Sculpture of numerous fine, concentric ridges.
Hinge area: Lunule heart-shaped; ligament strong, placed in groove; 3 cardinal teeth in each valve.
Pallial line & interior: Interior smooth, glossy; 2 small muscle scars connected by pallial line with large, angular sinus extending to center of shell.
Habitat: Near shore from 3.6 to 21.6 meters (2 to 12 fathoms); infaunal.
Localities: Entire.
Occurrence: Common.

Range: Virginia to Florida; Gulf states; Mexico; Bahamas.
Remarks: Pairs held together by strong ligament; commonly wash ashore in winter; often neat holes drilled by predatory gastropod present.

Elegant Dosinia
Dosinia elegans Conrad, 1846

Size: 50–76 mm.
Color: Ivory.
Shape: Lenticular, flattened; equivalve; inequilateral.
Ornament or sculpture: Sculpture of regular concentric ribs, fewer in number and heavier than in *D. discus*.
Hinge area: Umbones prominent; lunule small, partly submarginal; 3 cardinal teeth in each valve with lateral teeth present; left middle cardinal and right posterior cardinal bifid.
Pallial line & interior: 2 muscle scars connected by pallial line with long, angular sinus touching posterior scar; margins smooth.
Habitat: Offshore; infaunal.
Localities: Southern half of coast, more near south.
Occurrence: Uncommon beach shell.
Range: South Carolina; Florida; south Texas to Isla Mujeres; Yucatán.

Remarks: Inhabitant of Texas transitional zone, seldom found north of Big Shell on Padre Island; may be syn. of *D. concentrica* (Born, 1778); specimen figured in *SST*, p. 243, is *Cyclinella tenuis* (Récluz, 1852).

Subfamily GEMMINAE Dall, 1902

Genus *Gemma* Deshayes, 1853

Amethyst Gem Clam
Gemma cf. *G. purpurea* Lea, 1842

Subfamily CYCLININAE Frizzell, 1936

Genus *Cyclinella* Dall, 1902

Atlantic Cyclinella
Cyclinella tenuis (Récluz, 1852)

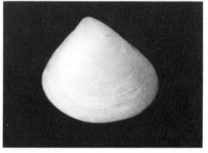

Size: 25–50 mm.
Color: Whitish.
Shape: Circular, flattened; equivalve; inequilateral.
Ornament or sculpture: Resembles *Dosinia* but smaller and more thin shelled; surface sculptured with very fine, irregular growth lines.
Hinge area: Submarginal hinge ligament; 3 cardinal teeth but no laterals as *Dosinia* have; right posterior tooth bifid.
Pallial line & interior: 2 muscle scars; anterior scar much nearer ventral margin than that of *Dosinia*; pallial sinus ascending, long, narrow; margins smooth.
Habitat: Inlet-influenced areas and bay margins; infaunal.
Localities: Entire, more to south.
Occurrence: Fairly common.
Range: Eastern United States; Texas; West Indies; Surinam; Brazil.
Remarks: Easily mistaken for *Dosinia* but much smaller.

Size: 3 mm.
Color: Whitish with purple on umbones and posterior areas.
Shape: Rounded trigonal.
Ornament or sculpture: Glossy with numerous, fine, concentric ribs.
Hinge area: Lunule large; 2 large teeth in left valve with socket between, 3 teeth in right valve.
Pallial line & interior: Small muscle scars; pallial sinus points upward, triangular; inner margin faintly crenulate.
Habitat: In shallow water, sandy bottom; infaunal.
Localities: Port Aransas area, probably other locations.
Occurrence: Uncommon in beach drift.
Range: Nova Scotia to Florida; Texas; Yucatán; Bahamas; introduced to Puget Sound.

Remarks: One of smallest bivalves; easily overlooked; tentative identity of figured specimens found in drift along Aransas Pass ship channel not checked by expert.

Subfamily CHIONINAE Frizzell, 1936

Genus *Chione* Megerle von Mühlfeld, 1811

Cross-Barred Venus
Chione cancellata (Linné, 1767)

Size: 25–27 mm.
Color: White to gray, often rayed with brown; interior glossy white with blue purple.
Shape: Ovate to subtrigonal; equivalve; inequilateral.
Ornament or sculpture: Surface sculptured with numerous strong, bladelike concentric ridges and many radial ribs; when concentric ridges beachworn, pattern appears very cancellate; heavy, porcelaneous.
Hinge area: Escutcheon long, smooth, V-shaped; lunule heart-shaped; 3 cardinal teeth in each valve; no anterior laterals.
Pallial line & interior: 2 muscle scars connected by pallial line with very small, triangular pallial sinus; margins crenulate.
Habitat: Open bays, bay margins, inlet-influenced areas; infaunal.

Localities: Entire, more to south.
Occurrence: Common.
Range: North Carolina to Florida; Texas; Gulf of Mexico to Quintana Roo; Costa Rica; West Indies; Brazil; Brazilian oceanic islands.
Remarks: Number of dead shells found in bay areas indicates species more abundant in past.

Lady-in-Waiting Venus
Chione intapurpurea (Conrad, 1849)

Size: 25–38 mm.
Color: Glossy white to cream, often with irregular brown marks; interior white or with purple splotch in posterior third.
Shape: Ovate to subtrigonal, inflated; equivalve; inequilateral.
Ornament or sculpture: Sculpture of numerous low, rounded concentric ribs; ribs marked with tiny serrations at lower edge that give interspaces beaded appearance; rib on posterior slope lamellate.
Hinge area: Lunule heart-shaped with raised lamellations; escutcheon with fine transverse lines; ligament exterior; 3 cardinal teeth in each valve, no laterals.
Pallial line & interior: 2 shiny muscle scars connected by pallial line with short, narrow, oblique sinus.
Habitat: Near shore, 3.6 to 21.6 meters (2 to 12 fathoms); infaunal.

Localities: Entire.
Occurrence: Fairly common beach shell.
Range: Chesapeake Bay to Florida; Texas; Yucatán; West Indies; Brazil.
Remarks: More readily found on Mexican Gulf beaches.

Subgenus *Lirophora* Conrad, 1863

Clench's Chione
Chione (Lirophora) clenchi Pulley, 1952

Size: 25–63 mm.
Color: Cream with irregular brown splotches, some rayed with brown.
Shape: Subtrigonal; equivalve; inequilateral.
Ornament or sculpture: Sculpture of 12 to 15 rounded concentric ribs; ribs not reflected dorsally or flattened on posterior slope; ribs sharply flexed along posterior slope, producing knobby ridge.
Hinge area: Umbones recurved forward; ligament sunken; escutcheon of moderate size, narrow, with faint growth lines; 3 cardinal teeth in each valve.
Pallial line & interior: Interior white, sometimes with purple or brown blotch under posterior slope; pallial line weak with small pallial sinus and 2 muscle scars; margin finely crenulate.

Habitat: Offshore; infaunal.
Localities: Entire, more to south.
Occurrence: Fairly common.
Range: Texas to Campeche, Campeche, Mexico.
Remarks: *C. latilirata* Conrad, 1841, may be same species, ribbing main difference; holotype collected off Port Isabel, Texas, ca. 1951, by L. A. Weisenhaus.

Subgenus *Timoclea* Brown, 1827

Gray Pygmy Venus
Chione (Timoclea) grus (Holmes, 1858)

Size: 6–9 mm.
Color: Grayish white, often with pink cast; interior with broad ray of purple at posterior end.
Shape: Oblong; inequivalve; inequilateral.
Ornament or sculpture: 30 to 40 fine, radial ribs crossed by finer, concentric threads; more heavily sculptured on posterior and anterior margins.
Hinge area: Lunule narrow, heart-shaped, colored brown; escutcheon narrow, sunken; 3 cardinal teeth in each valve.
Pallial line & interior: 2 muscle scars connected by weak pallial line with small, oblique sinus; margins crenulate.
Habitat: Offshore in intermediate shelf assemblage; sand and shell bottom; infaunal.

Localities: Central, south.
Occurrence: Uncommon in beach drift.
Range: North Carolina to Key West to Louisiana; Texas to Cabo Catoche, Mexico; Quintana Roo.

Genus *Mercenaria* Schumacher, 1817

Southern Quahog
Mercenaria campechiensis (Gmelin, 1791)

Size: 76–152 mm.
Color: Dirty gray to whitish; interior white, rarely with purple blotches; porcelaneous.
Shape: Ovate trigonal, inflated; equivalve; inequilateral.
Ornament or sculpture: Sculpture of numerous concentric growth lines, farther apart near beaks; shell very heavy.
Hinge area: Lunule as wide as long; 3 cardinals in each valve; left middle cardinal split.
Pallial line & interior: 2 muscle scars connected by pallial line with small, angular sinus.
Habitat: Offshore; infaunal.
Localities: Entire.
Occurrence: Common.
Range: Chesapeake Bay to Florida; Texas; Yucatán; Cuba.
Remarks: Not been used commercially as has its northern relative, *M. mercenaria.*

Texas Quahog
Mercenaria campechiensis texana (Dall, 1902)

Size: 76–127 mm.
Color: Dirty white, often with brown zigzag marks; interior white, occasionally marked with purple.
Shape: Ovate trigonal.
Ornament or sculpture: Surface sculptured with irregular, large concentric growth lines; central area of each valve glossy and smooth in older specimens; very heavy, porcelaneous.
Hinge area: Lunule three-fourths as wide as long; 3 cardinal teeth in each valve; left middle cardinal split.
Pallial line & interior: 2 muscle scars connected by pallial line with small, angular sinus; margin faintly crenulate.
Habitat: Open bays and inlet-influenced areas; infaunal.
Localities: Entire.
Occurrence: Fairly common.
Range: Northern Gulf of Mexico to Tampico, Tamaulipas, Mexico.
Remarks: Lives buried in bays; smooth-sided, elongated, pear-shaped siphonal holes observed while exposed during extremely low tide; during day, no siphon visible in opening, but just before sundown, as light was fading, two slender, white siphons would emerge and lie on substratum beside hole, quickly withdrawn when approached; can be used for chowder if

relocated in clear Gulf water so that it can filter enough water to remove flavor of muddy bay; shell has smoother disc than does its relative in Gulf; holotype collected by J. A. Singley at Corpus Christi Bay, Texas, in 1893.

Genus *Anomalocardia* Schumacher, 1817

Pointed Venus
Anomalocardia auberiana (Orbigny, 1842)

Size: 12–18 mm.
Color: Variable: from white to tan with brown rays; interior white with purplish brown at posterior margin.
Shape: Wedge-shaped; equivalve; inequilateral.
Ornament or sculpture: Glossy surface sculptured with rounded concentric ridges and very faint radial lines; posterior slope slightly rostrate.
Hinge area: Umbones small; lunule distinct; escutcheon depressed; 3 cardinal teeth in each valve; right anterior cardinal small and in horizontal position.
Pallial line & interior: 2 muscle scars connected by pallial line and small, angular sinus; margins crenulate.
Habitat: Both enclosed and open hypersaline lagoons; infaunal.
Localities: Entire, more to south.
Occurrence: Common.
Range: Southern half of Florida; Texas; Yucatán; Quintana Roo; Central America; West Indies; Brazil to Uruguay.

Remarks: Can withstand high salinity; one of few mollusks that can live in central Laguna Madre and Baffin Bay; syn. *A. cuneimeris* Conrad, 1846.

Family PETRICOLIDAE Deshayes, 1831

Genus *Petricola* Lamarck, 1801
Subgenus *Petricolaria* Stoliczka, 1870

False Angel Wing
Petricola (Petricolaria) pholadiformis (Lamarck, 1818)

Size: Up to 50 mm.
Color: White.
Shape: Elongate, somewhat cylindrical.
Ornament or sculpture: Sculpture of numerous radial ribs and fine growth lines, diminishing posteriorly on fragile shell; anterior ribs prominently scaled.
Hinge area: Umbones low, near anterior end; small, brown ligament just posterior to umbones; 3 cardinal teeth long, pointed in left valve, 2 in right.
Pallial line & interior: Both adductor muscle scars somewhat rounded; pallial sinus fairly narrow and deep with rounded end.
Habitat: Open-bay margins, inlet-influenced areas, near shore in clay banks; infaunal.
Localities: Entire.
Occurrence: Common.
Range: Gulf of St. Lawrence to Gulf of Mexico; Brazil to Uruguay.
Remarks: Easily confused with *Pholas*; check teeth.

Subgenus *Pseudoirus* Habe, 1951

Atlantic Rupellaria
Petricola (Pseudoirus) typica (Jonas, 1844)

Order MYOIDEA Stoliczka, 1870
Suborder MYINA Newell, 1965
Superfamily MYACEA Lamarck, 1809
Family MYIDAE Lamarck, 1809

Genus *Paramya* Conrad, 1861

Paramya subovata (Conrad, 1845)

Size: 25 mm.
Color: White.
Shape: Oblong, variable; inequilateral.
Ornament or sculpture: Rather heavy shell sculptured with irregularly spaced radial ribs, narrower over anterior area; valves gape posteriorly.
Hinge area: Umbones rounded, not prominent, curved forward; 3 cardinal teeth in left valve, 2 in right.
Pallial line & interior: Pallial sinus semicircular, somewhat longer than posterior adductor scar.
Habitat: Jetties and offshore; infaunal.
Localities: Central, south.
Occurrence: Fairly common.
Range: North Carolina to southern half of Florida; Texas; Yucatán; West Indies; Brazil.
Remarks: Shape of this coral- and rock-dwelling bivalve variable, conforming to dwelling place; [*Rupellaria typica*].

Size: 5–10 mm.
Color: Grayish white.
Shape: Subquadrate.
Ornament or sculpture: Concentric growth lines and microscopic granules near edge of valves.
Hinge area: Chondrophore in either valve.
Pallial line & interior: Polished; pallial line simple, hardly discernible; large, highly polished, pear-shaped muscle scar near dorsal area.
Habitat: Offshore; commensal with echiuroid worm, *Thalassema hartmani*.
Localities: East, central.
Occurrence: Uncommon.
Range: Delaware to Florida; Texas.
Remarks: Collected alive with echiuroid worms at entrance to Bolivar Roads Channel, Galveston, in May 1975 by Clyde A. Henry.

Family CORBULIDAE Lamarck, 1818
Subfamily CORBULINAE Gray, 1823

Genus *Corbula* Bruguière, 1797

Caribbean Corbula
Corbula cf. *C. caribaea* d'Orbigny,
1842

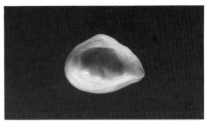

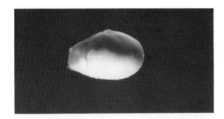

(completed second growth stage)

(first growth stage)

(mature)

(beginning second growth stage)

Size: 9 mm.
Color: White.
Shape: Subovoid, very solid; inequivalve; slightly inequilateral; posterior
acutely rostrate; anterior well rounded
and globose; dorsal margins nearly
straight and ventral margin excurved.
Ornament or sculpture: Irregular
concentric ridges and striae; larger

valve sculptured more regularly and deeply than other, with minute radiating striae in young.

Hinge area: Beaks small, not involute; umbones very convex, indistinctly angulated anteriorly, with sharp but not very prominent angle posteriorly; stout teeth.

Pallial line & interior: Simple; 2 small muscle scars.

Habitat: Muddy bottom in bays and offshore.

Localities: Entire.

Occurrence: Common.

Range: North Carolina; Florida; West Indies; Surinam to Brazil.

Remarks: Literature abounds with confusion concerning the genus *Corbula*; to add my bit: figured specimens may or may not be *C. caribaea*, syn. *C. swiftiana* C. B. Adams, 1852, and may be *C. barrattiana* C. B. Adams, 1852; group of figures helps explain dilemma.

Subgenus *Varicorbula* Grant & Gale, 1931

Oval Corbula
Corbula (Varicorbula) operculata
(Philippi, 1849)

Size: 9 mm.

Color: Whitish.

Shape: Subtrigonal, inflated; inequivalve.

Ornament or sculpture: Sculpture of strong, concentric ridges; right valve larger than left, more inflated, stronger sculpture.

Hinge area: Umbones high, almost central, curved in; right valve has single prominent cardinal tooth; left valve has corresponding socket; ligament internal.

Pallial line & interior: 2 small roundish muscle scars; pallial line well impressed; pallial sinus but slight sinuation in pallial line.

Habitat: Offshore, 36 to 62 meters (20 to 40 fathoms); infaunal.

Localities: Central, south.

Occurrence: Fairly common in beach drift.

Range: North Carolina to Gulf of Mexico; West Indies; northern and northeastern Brazil.

Remarks: Common outer-beach *Corbula*, sometimes found in bamboo-root clumps; commensal with Foraminifera; *C. krebsiana* C. B. Adams, 1852, may be same.

Superfamily GASTROCHAENACEA
 Gray, 1840
Family GASTROCHAENIDAE Gray,
 1840

Genus *Gastrochaena* Spengler, 1783

Atlantic Rocellaria
Gastrochaena hians (Gmelin, 1791)

Superfamily HIATELLACEA Gray,
 1824
Family HIATELLIDAE Gray, 1824

Genus *Hiatella* Daudin, 1801

Arctic Saxicave
Hiatella arctica (Linné, 1767)

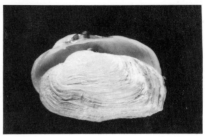

Size: 12–18 mm.
Color: White.
Shape: Petal-shaped.
Ornament or sculpture: Sculpture of
low, indistinct, fine, concentric lines;
posterior end large, rounded; entire
ventral-anterior end gaping to
accommodate foot.
Hinge area: Umbones low; hinge area
weak with 1 large toothlike structure in
umbonal cavity.
Pallial line & interior: Posterior
adductor scar large; anterior scar
degenerate; pallial sinus deep, angular.
Habitat: Offshore; infaunal.
Localities: Entire.
Occurrence: Uncommon in beach drift.
Range: Bermuda; North Carolina to
Florida; Texas; Yucatán; West Indies;
Surinam; northeastern and eastern
Brazil.
Remarks: Constructs hollow "cell" of
sand and bits of shell glued together in
which it lives; often found inside empty
pecten shells; [*Rocellaria hians*].

Size: 25 mm.
Color: Chalky white.
Shape: Irregularly oblong.
Ornament or sculpture: Sculpture of
coarse, irregular growth lines; weak
radial rib on posterior end, may be
scaled; posterior may gape.
Hinge area: Umbones close together
and about one-third back from anterior
end; teeth indefinite.
Pallial line & interior: Pallial line
discontinuous; sinus large but irregular.
Habitat: Inlet areas, hypersaline
lagoons, offshore; boring infaunal.
Localities: Entire.
Occurrence: Fairly common.
Range: Arctic seas to deep waters in
West Indies; Yucatán; Brazil; Pacific.
Remarks: Nestling and boring habits
cause shape and sculpture to vary
greatly.

Genus *Panopea* Menard de la Groye, 1807

Geoduck
Panopea bitruncata (Conrad, 1872)

Size: 127–228 mm.
Color: White.
Shape: Quadrate, elongated.
Ornament or sculpture: Sculpture of concentric, wavy growth lines; valves gape at both ends.
Hinge area: Umbones low, incurved, almost central; 1 large single, simple "tooth" and broad ledge to which ligament attached.
Pallial line & interior: Anterior adductor muscle scar elongated; posterior rounded, small; pallial sinus short, rounded.
Habitat: Offshore and inlet areas; boring infaunal.
Localities: Port Aransas, south.
Occurrence: Rare beach shell.
Range: North Carolina to Florida and south Texas.
Remarks: Seldom found alive or dead because lives so deep in substratum that valves rarely wash out of burrows; live juvenile specimens found in Aransas Pass channel during very extreme, extended low tide.

Suborder PHOLADINA Newell, 1965
Superfamily PHOLADACEA Lamarck, 1809
Family PHOLADIDAE Lamarck, 1809
Subfamily PHOLADINAE Lamarck, 1809

Genus *Pholas* Linné, 1758
Subgenus *Thovana* Gray, 1847

Campeche Angel Wing
Pholas (Thovana) campechiensis (Gmelin, 1791)

Size: Up to 128 mm.
Color: White.
Shape: Subelliptical.
Ornament or sculpture: Thin, fragile shell sculptured with laminate, concentric ridges and radial ribs; sculpture becomes weaker posteriorly; shells gape; shells rounded at both ends.
Hinge area: Umbones prominent, located near anterior fourth of shell, covered by double septate umbonal reflections; apophyses delicate, short, broad, projecting beneath umbo at sharp posterior angle; 3 accessory plates: nearly rectangular protoplax, transverse mesoplax, elongate metaplax.

Pallial line & interior: Adductor muscle scars and pallial line well marked; pallial sinus wide, extending anteriorly almost two-thirds of distance to umbo.
Habitat: Offshore in wood and clay; boring infaunal.
Localities: Entire.
Occurrence: Fairly common.
Range: North Carolina to Gulf states; Mexico; Costa Rica; West Indies; Surinam; Brazil to Uruguay; Senegal to Liberia.
Remarks: Common in beach drift but seldom found alive; at times found in wood on outer beaches; distinguished by comblike umbonal reflection; figured specimen filled with cotton.

Genus *Barnea* Risso, 1826

Fallen Angel Wing
Barnea truncata (Say, 1822)

Size: 71 mm.
Color: White.
Shape: Elongate elliptical.
Ornament or sculpture: Rather thin shell sculptured with radial ribs and concentric ridges; concentric ridges have lamella anteriorly, becoming weaker toward posterior end; radial ribs lacking on posterior slope; imbrications formed where concentric ridges cross radial ribs; shell beaked anteriorly and truncate posteriorly.
Hinge area: Umbones prominent, near anterior third; apophysis narrow, long, bladelike, curved; protoplax lanceolate, with posterior nucleus and definite growth lines.

Pallial line & interior: Pallial line and muscle scars well marked; pallial sinus almost as wide as shell is high, extending about halfway to umbones.
Habitat: In clay bottoms of bays; boring infaunal.
Localities: Central.
Occurrence: Fairly common.
Range: Massachusetts Bay to southern Florida; Texas; Surinam; eastern Brazil; Senegal.
Remarks: Siphons capable of extending 10 to 12 times length of shell; animal cannot withdraw into shell and usually lives in deep burrows in clay but known to live in wood also.

Genus *Cyrtopleura* Tryon, 1862
Subgenus *Scobinopholas* Grant & Gale, 1931

Angel Wing
Cyrtopleura (Scobinopholas) costata (Linné, 1758)

Size: 177 mm.
Color: White.
Shape: Elongate oval.
Ornament or sculpture: Rather light shell sculptured with concentric ridges and strong radial ribs that extend entire length of shell; where ribs cross concentric line, imbrications formed, stronger on anterior and posterior slopes.
Hinge area: Umbones prominent, located near anterior fourth of shell; umbones well separated from raised umbonal reflections; protoplax triangular in outline, mostly chitinous;

mesoplax calcareous; apophyses large, spoon-shaped, hollow at upper end.
Pallial line & interior: Anterior and posterior muscle scars fairly well marked, but pallial sinus not evident.
Habitat: Open-bay margins, inlet-influenced areas; boring infaunal.
Localities: Entire.
Occurrence: Common.
Range: Massachusetts to Florida; Texas; Mexico; West Indies; Surinam; Brazilian coast to Paraná.
Remarks: Bores into clay substratum in bays to depth of about 46 centimeters (18 inches); inability to withdraw into shell makes it very susceptible to changes of salinity; [*Pholas costata*].

Subfamily MARTESIINAE Grant & Gale, 1931

Genus *Martesia* G. B. Sowerby I, 1824
Subgenus *Martesia* s.s.

Fragile Martesia
Martesia (Martesia) fragilis Verrill & Bush, 1890

Size: 18 mm.
Color: White.
Shape: Pear-shaped.
Ornament or sculpture: Valves divided into 2 sections by shallow umbonal-ventral sulcus; anterior part sculptured with concentric, denticulated ridges and weak radial ribs; posterior part sculptured with smooth, rounded ridges; truncated beaks gape; shell rounded, closed posteriorly.
Hinge area: Umbones prominent, located near anterior end of shell in adults; mesoplax circular to oval, depressed with strong concentric sculpture; metaplax long, narrow, pointed anteriorly, wider and rounded posteriorly; apophyses long, thin, extending under umbones anteriorly at angle.
Pallial line & interior: Muscle scars strong; pallial sinus wide, deep, extending almost to umbonal-ventral ridge.
Habitat: Pelagic in floating wood; boring infaunal.
Localities: Entire.
Occurrence: Common.
Range: Bermuda; Virginia south through Gulf of Mexico; West Indies to Brazil; Surinam; Pacific coast of Mexico; Indo-Pacific.
Remarks: Easily confused with *M. striata*; however, mesoplax depressed, has concentric sculpture, and has sharply keeled edges.

Subgenus *Particoma* Bartsch & Rehder, 1945

Wedge-Shaped Martesia
Martesia (Particoma) cuneiformis (Say, 1822)

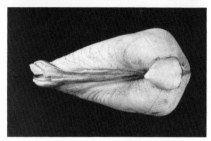

pallial sinus broad, extending anteriorly beyond umbonal-ventral ridge.
Habitat: Pelagic in wood; boring infaunal.
Localities: Entire.
Occurrence: Fairly common.
Range: Southeastern United States; Texas; West Indies; Brazil; Pacific Panama.
Remarks: Easily confused with *Diplothyra smithii* Tryon, 1862, unless characteristic wedge-shaped mesoplax present; material in which animal bores readily affects shape of genus, causing some problem in identification.

Genus *Diplothyra* Tryon, 1862

Oyster Piddock
Diplothyra smithii Tryon, 1862

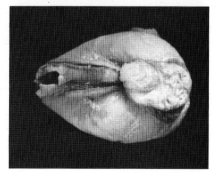

Size: 12–21 mm.
Color: White.
Shape: Pear-shaped.
Ornament or sculpture: Valves divided into parts by narrow, umbonal-ventral sulcus; anterior part sculptured with concentric, denticulated ridges; posterior part sculptured with smooth, rounded, concentric ridges, weak growth lines; shell gapes anteriorly, rounded, closed posteriorly.
Hinge area: Umbones prominent, located near anterior end of shell; umbonal reflection small, adpressed, not free; mesoplax cuneiform, or wedge-shaped, with median groove and radiating growth lines; metaplax long, narrow, divided; apophyses long, thin, almost parallel with umbonal-ventral ridge.
Pallial line & interior: Muscle scars well marked; posterior adductor scar long, oval; anterior scar kidney-shaped;

Size: 15 mm.
Color: White.
Shape: Pear-shaped.
Ornament or sculpture: Divided into 2 parts by umbonal-ventral sulcus; anterior part triangular in shape, sculptured by fine, close-set, wavy, concentric ridges and numerous weak radial ribs; posterior part has only growth lines; widely gaping anteriorly; rounded, closed posteriorly.
Hinge area: Umbones prominent, near anterior fourth of shell; umbones imbedded in callum that extends posteriorly on either side of mesoplax; apophyses long, thin, fragile; large chondrophore in left valve; mesoplax divided into concentrically sculptured posterior section and wrinkled anterior section; mesoplax and hypoplax forked posteriorly.
Pallial line & interior: Adductor scars large; pallial sinus broad, deep, extending anteriorly past umbonal-ventral ridge.
Habitat: High-salinity oyster reefs; boring infaunal.
Localities: Entire.
Occurrence: Common.
Range: Massachusetts south to Daytona Beach and Sanibel Island, Florida; west to Texas and Surinam.
Remarks: Similar in appearance to *Martesia cuneiformis* but not found in wood, preferring shell and coquina rock; bores into oyster shell but not commercially damaging; [*Martesia smithii*].

Subfamily JOUANNETIINAE Tryon, 1862

Genus *Jouannetia* Des Moulins, 1818
Quilling's Jouannetia
Jouannetia quillingi R. D. Turner, 1955

Size: 21 mm.
Color: White to gray.
Shape: Globose, pear-shaped.
Ornament or sculpture: Valves divided into 2 parts by umbonal-ventral sulcus; anterior part triangular and sculptured with numerous laminate, imbricate, concentric ridges and weak radial ribs; shell constricted at sulcus; posterior part sculptured with thin, concentric ridges and growth lines; ridges bear long, curved spines.
Hinge area: Umbones prominent, near anterior third of shell; umbonal reflections free, raised; callum extends dorsally between beaks, on left valve enlarged to form covering for anterior adductor muscle; mesoplax small, wedge-shaped; chondrophore on left valve.
Pallial line & interior: Muscle scars barely visible; pallial sinus extends anteriorly to umbonal-ventral ridge.
Habitat: In wood and calcareous rock offshore, pelagic; boring infaunal.
Localities: Central.
Occurrence: Uncommon to rare.
Range: North Carolina to Lake Worth, Florida; Texas.
Remarks: Only recently found on Texas coast in floating wood.

Family TEREDINIDAE Rafinesque, 1815
Subfamily TEREDININAE Rafinesque, 1815

Genus *Teredo* Linné, 1758

Bartsch's Shipworm
Teredo bartschi Clapp, 1923

(after R. D. Turner, *A survey and illustrated catalogue of the Teredinidae* [Cambridge, Mass.: Harvard Univ. Mus. Comp. Zool., 1966], p. 147)

Size: 27 mm.
Color: Pallets white.
Shape: Stalk long; blade short.
Ornament or sculpture: Blade deeply excavated at top.
Hinge area: None.
Pallial line & interior: None.
Habitat: Wood borer; infaunal.
Localities: Entire.
Occurrence: Fairly common.
Range: Bermuda; South Carolina to northern half of Florida and Texas; introduced to Baja California.
Remarks: Pallets, not shell, used in identification.

Genus *Lyrodus* Binney, 1870

Stalked Shipworm
Lyrodus pedicellatus (Quatrefages, 1849) [See *SST*, p. 258]

Subfamily BANKIINAE Turner, 1966

Genus *Bankia* Gray, 1842
Subgenus *Bankiella* Bartsch, 1921

Gould's Shipworm
Bankia (Bankiella) gouldi (Bartsch, 1908)

(after Turner 1966, p. 247)

Size: 27 mm.
Color: White.
Shape: Pallet elongate.
Ornament or sculpture: Blade composed of numerous conelike elements on central stalk.
Hinge area: None.
Pallial line & interior: None.
Habitat: In wood, mangroves; boring infaunal.
Localities: Entire.
Occurrence: Common.
Range: New Jersey to Florida; Texas; Central America; West Indies; Brazil; Pacific coast of Mexico.
Remarks: Shells helpful in identification only when used in conjunction with pallets.

Subclass ANOMALODESMATA Dall, 1889
Order PHOLADOMYOIDEA Newell, 1965
Superfamily PANDORACEA Rafinesque, 1815
Family PANDORIDAE Rafinesque, 1815

Genus *Pandora* Bruguière, 1797
Subgenus *Clidophora* Carpenter, 1864

Say's Pandora
Pandora (Clidophora) trilineata Say, 1822

Size: 18–25 mm.
Color: White to cream; interior pearly.
Shape: Semilunar, flat; inequivalve; inequilateral.
Ornament or sculpture: Flat, compressed valves sculptured with microscopic, concentric growth lines; left valve has radial ridge along posterior slope; strong ridge along hinge margin.
Hinge area: Umbones tiny, near rounded anterior end; hinge internal just below umbones; lamellar plates replace teeth.
Pallial line & interior: 2 small, round adductor muscles; pallial line smple, discontinuous.
Habitat: Inlet areas, open-sound and lagoon centers in clayey sediments; infaunal.
Localities: Entire.
Occurrence: Common.
Range: Cape Hatteras to Florida; Texas.

Family LYONSIIDAE Fischer, 1887

Genus *Lyonsia* Turton, 1822

Florida Lyonsia
Lyonsia floridana Conrad, 1848

Size: 16 mm.
Color: White, translucent.
Shape: Elongate, rather tear-shaped; inequivalve; inequilateral.
Ornament or sculpture: Thin shell sculptured with fine growth lines; valves gape posteriorly.
Hinge area: Umbones tiny, pointed; no teeth; small groove posterior to umbones houses ligament.
Pallial line & interior: 2 adductor muscle scars; pallial line indistinct.
Habitat: Open-bay margins, inlet areas, in grass beds; infaunal.
Localities: Central.
Occurrence: Fairly common.
Range: West coast of Florida; Texas; Surinam.
Remarks: Byssal attachment.

Family PERIPLOMATIDAE Dall, 1895

Genus *Periploma* Schumacher, 1816

Unequal Spoon Clam
Periploma margaritaceum (Lamarck, 1801)

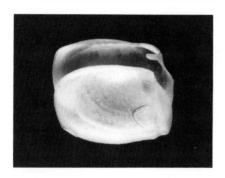

Size: 18–25 mm.
Color: White, translucent.
Shape: Subquadrate; inequivalve; inequilateral.
Ornament or sculpture: Sculpture of fine, concentric growth lines on rather fragile shell; posterior margin very truncate; low keel from umbones to anterior ventral margin.
Hinge area: Umbones small, near posterior end; ligament internal, located in spoon-shaped "tooth" in each valve.
Pallial line & interior: 2 small adductor muscle scars; pallial sinus broad, short, strongly defined.
Habitat: Open-sound, open-lagoon centers, inlet areas in sandy bottoms; infaunal.
Localities: Entire.
Occurrence: Common.
Range: South Carolina to Florida; Texas to Mexico; Costa Rica; West Indies; Brazil.
Remarks: Sporadically on outer beach in large numbers; valves often with holes bored by gastropod; syn. *P. inequale* (C. B. Adams, 1842).

Class SCAPHOPODA Bronn, 1862

Family DENTALIIDAE Gray, 1834

Genus *Dentalium* Linné, 1758
Subgenus *Paradentalium* Cotton &
Godfrey, 1933

Texas Tusk
Dentalium (Paradentalium) texasianum
Philippi, 1849

Occurrence: Common.
Range: North Carolina to Texas;
Yucatán.
Remarks: Holotype collected by
F. Roemer near Galveston, Texas, ca.
1846; Petersen examined live specimens
and noted enormous amount of
variation in population of West Bay off
Galveston Island.

(apex)

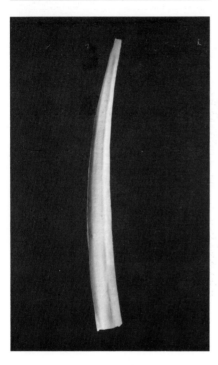

Size: 18–35 mm.
Color: White.
Shape: Tapering cylinder; curved.
Ornament or sculpture: Hexagonal in
cross section with 6 main ribs
interspaced with numerous cordlike
riblets on broad interspaces; apical pipe
clearly visible unless tip broken off.
Aperture: Hexagonal.
Habitat: Open-bay margins, inlets,
channel in stiff clay sediments; semi-
infaunal.
Localities: Entire.

Subgenus *Antalis* H. & A. Adams, 1954

Dentalium cf. *(Antalis)* sp. A & B

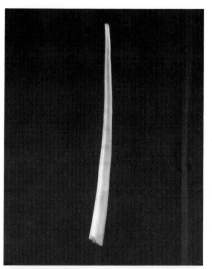

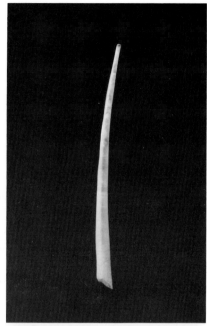

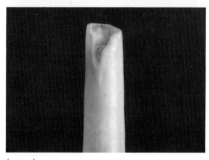

(apex)

(apex)

Size: Up to 28 mm.
Color: Whitish to pale amber.
Shape: Very slender, tapered cylinder; curved.
Ornament or sculpture: Microscopic longitudinal ribs at apical end of delicate shell; remainder of shell smooth except for growth rings; growth rings stronger than in *D.* cf. *(Laevidentalium)* sp. C; apical slit; some adult shells do not have microscopic lines.

Aperture: Round, simple.
Habitat: Inlet areas[?]; semi-infaunal.
Localities: Central, south, probably entire.
Occurrence: Fairly common.
Range: Not defined.
Remarks: 2 specimens and details of apexes figured; may or may not be same species; I have examined some of same size, shape, and color which are completely smooth with apical slit, some with apical ribs and slit, and others with apical ribs and no slit; previously all *Dentaliums* in Texas

without hexagonal cross section and heavy ribs of *D. texasianum* reported as being one species, *D. eboreum* Conrad, 1846; Conrad described *D. eboreum* as having microscopic apical striae but *no* slit; if absence of slit in those I have examined is natural and not due to breakage, they could be *D. eboreum*; however, those with slit do not fit that description.

Subgenus *Laevidentalium* Cossmann, 1888

Dentalium cf. *(Laevidentalium)* sp. C

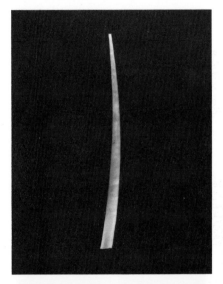

(apex)

Size: Up to 37 mm.
Color: White.
Shape: Tapered cylinder; curved.
Ornament or sculpture: Smooth except for faint growth rings; no apical slit; cross section round.
Aperture: Round, simple.
Habitat: Inlet areas and near shore; semi-infaunal.
Localities: Central, south.
Occurrence: Fairly common.
Range: Not defined.
Remarks: Shell identified as *D. eboreum* in Andrews 1971 and referred to by other Texas malacologists as *D. eboreum* Conrad, 1846, but larger and has less definite growth rings; examination under microscope shows absence of longitudinal apical ribs typical of *D. eboreum*.

Family SIPHONODENTALIIDAE Simroth, 1894

Genus *Cadulus* Philippi, 1844
Subgenus *Gadila* Gray, 1847

Cadulus cf. *(Gadila)* sp. A

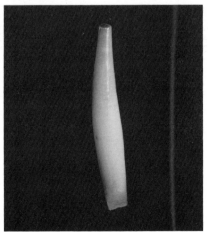

(apex)

Size: Up to 8 mm.
Color: White, smooth, glossy.
Shape: Cylinder; swollen in middle, tapering toward each end.
Ornament or sculpture: Smooth, polished.
Aperture: Round, simple.
Habitat: Near shore; semi-infaunal.
Localities: Entire.
Occurrence: Fairly common.
Range: Not determined.
Remarks: Shell mistakenly identified as *C. carolinensis* Bush, 1885, in Andrews 1971 and other literature on Texas shallow-water mollusks; typical "small, distinct notches, two on each side," described by Bush, absent in this small species, often abundant in beach drift; however, typical *C. carolinensis* found in deeper offshore waters; in addition to notches, has more oblique aperture than do specimens which wash up on beach.

Class CEPHALOPODA Cuvier, 1797

Subclass COLEOIDEA Bather, 1888
Order SEPIOIDEA Naef, 1916
Family SPIRULIDAE Owen, 1836

Genus *Spirula* Lamarck, 1799

Common Spirula
Spirula spirula (Linné, 1758)

Size: Animal 55 mm, shell 25 mm.
Color: Shell porcelaneous white; animal light brown.
Description: Closely coiled and chambered shell enclosed in posterior end of cylindrical body; 2 folds cover coiled shell, visible dorsally and ventrally but completely enclosed within mantle; posterior end of body truncate with 2 lateral fins; circular disc between fins emits light; 2 eyes in large head protrude beyond mantle edges; arms short, stout, pointed, with 4 rows of suckers; tentacles short with numerous rows of minute suckers.
Habitat: Offshore in deep waters.
Localities: Entire.
Occurrence: Common.
Range: Worldwide.
Remarks: Coiled shell often on outer beaches by thousands; normal position for animal is vertical with arms hanging down; living mollusk seldom seen.

Order TEUTHOIDEA Naef, 1916
Suborder MYOPSIDA Orbigny, 1840
Family LOLIGINIDAE Orbigny, 1841

Genus *Loliguncula* Steenstrup, 1881

Thumbstall Squid
Loliguncula brevis (Blainville, 1823)

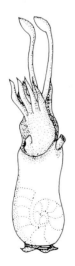

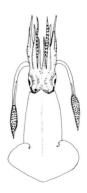

(after F. W. Lane, *Kingdom of the octopus* [New York: Sheridan House, 1960], p. 14)

(after G. L. Voss, *Bull. Marine Sci. Gulf & Caribbean* 5[2]:113 [1956])

Size: 75 mm.
Color: Cream with numerous reddish brown spots uniformly distributed over dorsal and ventral surfaces except for ventral surfaces of fins; narrow line down middle of back.
Description: Short and chunky with broad round fins about half length of body; tentacles long, slender with clublike ends; arms short, dorsal pair shortest.
Habitat: Bays and near shore; salinities of 17 to 30 ppt.
Localities: Entire.
Occurrence: Common.
Range: Maryland to Florida; Gulf of Mexico; Caribbean; South America to Río de la Plata.
Remarks: Moves out of bays and a few miles offshore during January and February; edible but primarily used for bait.

Genus *Loligo* Lamarck, 1798
Subgenus *Doryteuthis* Naef, 1912

Plee's Striped Squid
Loligo (Doryteuthis) pleii (Blainville, 1823)

(after Voss 1956, fig. b, p. 117)

Size: Up to 20.3 cm.
Color: Cream with long, narrow, wavy maroon lines running along side of mantle; small, maroon dots on remainder of mantle.

Description: Slender with large fins more than half of body length; males with large reddish flame markings on under side of body; arms short; pen with straight, thickened sides.
Habitat: Offshore at depths of 13 to 46 meters (7 to 25 fathoms).
Localities: Entire.
Occurrence: Common offshore.
Range: Tropical waters from Bermuda and south Florida; Gulf of Mexico; Caribbean Sea; Guianas.
Remarks: Prefers salinities greater than 30 ppt. but often caught in trawls with *Loliguncula brevis*; *Loligo plealeii* Lesueur, 1821, better known than any loliginid squid; however, in northwest Gulf of Mexico generally found at depths of 37 to 183 meters (20 to 100 fathoms) with salinities greater than 33 ppt.

Order OCTOPODA Leach, 1817
Suborder INCIRRATA Grimpe, 1916
Family OCTOPODIDAE Orbigny, 1840
Subfamily OCTOPODINAE Grimpe, 1921

Genus *Octopus* Cuvier, 1797

Pygmy Octopus
Octopus joubini Robson, 1929

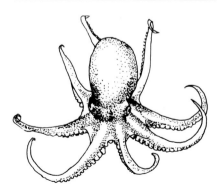

Size: 120 to 152 mm.
Color: Reddish brown with several large white pimples around eye.
Description: Small with short, relatively

equal-length arms; mating arm of male has fairly large spoon-shaped organ at tip.
Habitat: Shallow water, sandy bottom to about 9 meters (5 fathoms).
Localities: Entire.
Occurrence: Fairly common.
Range: Georgia south to Gulf of Mexico; Caribbean to Guianas.
Remarks: Often lives in old clam shells; lifespan about 1 year.

Common Atlantic Octopus
Octopus vulgaris Lamarck, 1798

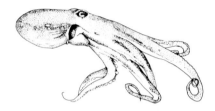

Size: 307–900 mm.
Color: Variable but commonly mottled reddish brown, white, and tan.
Description: Chunky with stout arms, upper pair always shortest; mating arm of male shorter with minute spoon-shaped organ at tip; may weigh 10 pounds.
Habitat: All types of bottom in shallow water to outer edge of continental shelf.
Localities: Entire.
Occurrence: Fairly common.
Range: Worldwide.
Remarks: Among rocks on jetties and sea walls; lives 1 or 2 years; males usually die following mating; females, after clusters of eggs, which it broods, are hatched.

Index